From Disgrace to Dignity

From Disgrace to Dignity

Redemption in the Life of Willie Rico Johnson

CLEMENS BARTOLLAS

CASCADE *Books* • Eugene, Oregon

FROM DISGRACE TO DIGNITY
Redemption in the Life of Willie Rico Johnson

Cascade Books
An Imprint of Wipf and Stock Publishers
199 W. 8th Ave., Suite 3
Eugene, OR 97401

www.wipfandstock.com

PAPERBACK ISBN: 978-1-5326-4714-7
HARDCOVER ISBN: 978-1-5326-4715-4
EBOOK ISBN: 978-1-5326-4716-1

Cataloguing-in-Publication data:

Names: Bartollas, Clemens, author.

Title: From disgrace to dignity : redemption in the life of Willie Rico Johnson / Clemens Bartollas.

Description: Eugene, OR: Cascade Books, 2019 | Series: if applicable | Includes bibliographical references

Identifiers: ISBN 978-1-5326-4714-7 (paperback) | ISBN 978-1-5326-4715-4 (hardcover) | ISBN 978-1-5326-4716-1 (ebook)

1. Muslim converts. 2. Black Muslims—Biography. 3. African Americans—Biography.

Classification: BP52 .B375 2019 (print) | BP52 (ebook)

Manufactured in the U.S.A.   DECEMBER 26, 2018

Bertha Johnson, my loving mother

Contents

Preface ix

Acknowledgments xix

1 Overview of the Vice Lords 1

2 Mommy's Little Man 14

3 Little Rico—A Terror in the Community 24

4 Early Prison Years and Survival 38

5 Beliefs and Practices of Islam—The First Redemptive Script 50

6 Falling Off the Wagon 80

7 Going Back to Prison 87

8 Readjustment to Prison, Leadership,
   and Influence on Others 101

9 Discouragement, Discouragement, and Discouragement 116

10 Tamms—A Nightmare 120

11 Paroled at Last 124

12 A Godfather in Action 128

13 Some Questions to Ponder 135

References 147

Preface

This biography is directed toward several audiences. First is the general public, which always likes a good gangster story; included in this group are parents who have an interest in gangs because they are afraid their children may become involved in them. Then there are the professionals who work with gangs, for they no doubt will find Willie Rico Johnson's story helpful in their efforts to understand gangs and their members. Additionally, college students who are studying criminal justice, sociology, or urban studies will find the history of a leader of one of the largest gangs in the nation relevant to their work. Finally, the story will interest more than thirty thousand members of the Vice Lords as well as those involved with other gangs. All will be intrigued by the path one of their own has followed and how his life has turned out.

Uniqueness and Relevance of This Biography

As I began writing this biography, I realized that it would be unique in a number of ways from other books on street or prison gangs.

- This volume is the first full-length biography featuring the life of a gang leader. There have been other biographies of gang members, some of which are quite useful in understanding gangs, but none has such an in-depth focus.
- This study includes interviews and statements from people who have been part of Rico's life up to the present day, including members of his gang and on occasion other gangs.

It examines Rico Johnson over the course of many years—from his birth onward—as he has gone about his daily life in Chicago.

- This biography is noteworthy in that it addresses the issue of redemption as it has occurred in Rico's life.

- This book tells the story of a man who set out to be the leader of the Vice Lords and shows how he was able to accomplish that goal. Put another way, it examines the processes of becoming a leader of a major urban gang and reveals the price that must be paid for choosing such a path.

- In its exposition of gang life in urban America, this volume offers policy makers key insights on urban survival. These insights may point to general solutions to the problems of poverty, single-parent families, and urban housing, all of which may be valuable in restructuring governance and policy-making in urban areas. The biography also shows why early exposure to the juvenile justice system so often leads to further involvement in the justice system later in life.

- Finally, this biography describes how gangs are structured, how they are ruled, and how they are woven into the larger social fabric of their immediate communities and the city at large. This knowledge should prove useful in designing programs that truly work and helping youths to either avoid gangs altogether or disentangle themselves from their current gang affiliations.

Redemption: The Major Theme of This Biography

One of the notable aspects of this biography is that it portrays redemption as it took place in Rico Johnson's life. The dictionary defines *redemption* as the act of making something better or more acceptable, and in a larger religious context, it is the action of saving or being saved from error, evil, or sin.

The theme of redemption is not unique to Rico's life. An article in the December 26, 2016 edition of the *Los Angeles Times* related the story of Melvin Farmer, an original member of the Crips (one of the rivals of the Vice Lords), who was working in his neighborhood to help youths deal with poverty, gangs, and unemployment. He was seeking to turn his life around and become a force for positive change in others' lives.[1] This is the same vision that Rico is pursuing today.

But redemption has not always guided Rico's life nor Melvin Farmer's. Before Rico went to prison and after he was paroled in 1980, he continued to commit crimes. At times, he hurt others. He was convinced that he had to deal harshly with certain people and that failing to do so would show weakness and put his status as a leader in jeopardy among his peers.

Following his imprisonment at Stateville Correctional Center, Rico became convinced that adopting Islam would supply what was missing in his life. With an able mentor, he became committed to the philosophy, practices, and expected behaviors of the Muslim faith. His own conversion to Islam led him to spearhead the conversion of the Conservative Vice Lords, both those who were imprisoned and those in the community, and he himself became a minister of the faith. The prayers and belief statements of the Vice Lords are presented later in this book.

Yet despite his religious conversion, when Rico was released from prison in the 1980s he literally returned to the streets, forsaking his newfound beliefs and committing whatever crimes he had to in order to become king of the hill. In a few years, his luck ran out, and he was apprehended and returned to the Illinois Department of Corrections with a long sentence.

Significantly, after he returned to prison he climbed back on the wagon once again, reaffirming his commitment to Allah and Muslim practices. He had to learn a more mature expression of the Islamic faith and beliefs, a gradual process that has taken place since the late 1970s. Was his redemptive true and lasting? The passage of time indicates it has been.

1. Campbell, "Searching for Redemption."

Another aspect of Rico's redemptive script is the positive effect that he had on other inmates as a minister during his incarceration. When a number of the inmates he worked with were released, they turned away from drugs and crime and have since attempted to improve their communities—some of them for twenty or thirty years. Over a decade or more, numerous individuals whom Rico counseled have maintained a crime-free and drug-free lifestyle.

Rico has continued to express and promote this redemptive philosophy since his release from prison in August 2012. As he put it, his goal is "to save the children."[2] He believes his life's mission is to make a difference in the lives of the young, so that they will not continue their involvement in crime and drugs and waste years in prison as he did. Other leaders in the community who began as gang members have turned their lives around as well and now feel compelled, just as Rico does, to assist others in avoiding the pitfalls they themselves have faced.

Minister Rico has in some ways succeeded where others have failed, and this biography explores the character traits and actions that have led to his success. For example, he is engaged in an outreach program to feed families in the community and now provides meals for up to 150 families on a daily basis. He also takes care of organizational matters with the Vice Lords and responds to inquiries from individuals in the community. Sometimes, this entails counseling the people; on other occasions, he plays the role of the godfather as seen in traditional gang and organized crime circles.

Since his release, Rico has found various ways to be a positive force in others' lives. To cite one instance, I have taken my students with me on several occasions when I have interviewed him, and if they are African American youths, Rico has confronted them with pointed questions: "What do you plan to do for the community?

---

2. Unless otherwise indicated, all direct quotes from Willie Rico Johnson are from my interviews with him on the following occasions: September 2012 and most Mondays in 2012, 2013, and 2014. Most interviews took place over the phone, but some did take place face to face in Chicago.

What changes do you need to make in your life to be the best person possible?"

Redemption has traditionally been described as being saved from sin, error, or evil. In Christian theology, it is typically seen as the act or process of being delivered from sin. It is accomplished by Jesus Christ through his atonement, and to be redeemed requires repentance and a desire to be a new person in Christ.

In this biography, the discussion of redemption is expanded to another religion—Islam—and to the dynamics of one individual's life—Rico Johnson's. We can extend the definition and meaning of redemption to a process that is multidimensional and more than linear. One can argue that *redemption* is a much better word than *rehabilitation* to describe the process of genuine change in a criminal's life.

One of the lessons I have learned from researching and writing this biography is that redemption can be divided into a set of processes. Redemption, in the context referred to here, encompasses the following stages:

1. Desiring life change. One has a genuine wish to change, coupled with a regret or sorrow for what one has done. We can refer to this as repentance, or a desire to walk away from old behaviors and attitudes.

2. Doing something about it. This change process may be reflected in behavioral change. An example would be the lifer in a Colorado prison whose desire for reformation in his life was expressed in training dogs for children, especially those who are handicapped. He and other inmates have trained some 200 dogs to work with such children.

3. Finding support and encouragement from others. Even if a person is determined to change and is finding ways to demonstrate a commitment to redemption, it is nearly impossible to sustain the change process without ongoing support from peers and others.

4. Falling off the wagon. Almost everyone who wants to change occasionally falls off the wagon, whether by drinking, taking

drugs, smoking, or indulging in other addictions. Intervention by support persons may be required to help individuals pick themselves up and go on.

5. Becoming steadfast and maturing in a new way of life. As someone who sees himself or herself as a new person goes on, the task is to grow and become steadfast in the new faith or way of seeing the world.

6. Avoiding recidivism. Many delinquents and criminals say that they want to stay away from crime, not unlike students who have struggled in school but declare they are determined to turn their schoolwork around. They feel that they want to change, yet somehow, they always end up where they started. For delinquents and criminals, this can mean committing more crime; being convicted in a court of law; or ending up in an institution, perhaps for the remainder of their lives. For a gang member, it may mean going back to selling drugs and perhaps winding up in the graveyard.

I believe it is redemption rather than rehabilitation that we desire for those who violate the law. Rico's ability to transform himself, to generate a new "me," certainly demonstrates that criminals can change, even the leaders of the largest gangs in the United States. This is not a novel concept but has been explored by some of the leading criminologists in the country. For example, Shadd Maruna has compared and contrasted the stories of ex-convicts who are actively involved in criminal behavior with those who are turning from crime and drug use.[3] Criminological and psychological thought suggests that success in reform depends on providing rehabilitative opportunities that reinforce a generative script.

Accordingly, I have concluded that if the redemptive experience is real, it will last; it will be expressed in more and more areas of one's life; and there will be a maturation process as time goes by. I invite readers to follow the path of Rico's life and judge for themselves whether his redemption is real.

3. Maruna, "Redemption Scrips and Desistance."

Gang Background

I am no stranger to the world of gangs. In 1961, I worked with a white juvenile gang near Newark, New Jersey. I got the job after my predecessor was assaulted (his attackers cut him in the chest and warned him that if he did not resign, they would kill him). I had no problems that year, but I did not return to working with juveniles and adults involved in gangs until later in the sixties. From 1969 to 1973, I worked in varying capacities in a maximum-security facility for older juveniles.

In 1973, I began my academic career in North Carolina, but two years later, when I accepted a position in Illinois, I again became involved in the gang world. I visited the Illinois prisons on a regular basis and developed relationships among lower-level members in several African American gangs.

Then in 1981, when I began teaching at the University of Iowa, I became involved with a gang, the Unknown Vice Lords, and their leader, Willie Lloyd. He and other Vice Lords were incarcerated in an Iowa prison, and a colleague and I visited the prison, spending most of our time talking with Lloyd.

We briefly considered doing a biography of his life, a project in which he was quite interested. Throughout the 1990s, Dr. Nehemiah Russell introduced me to a number of gang leaders, chiefly Larry Hoover of the Gangster Disciples and Willie Rico Johnson of the Vice Lords. I began to visit them in prison and even gave testimony in several of their parole hearings. Furthermore, I participated in Russell's Gang Deactivation Program at Englewood High School in Chicago. In the 2000s, I worked with a youth gang in Iowa whose members had been involved in a murder. And during my thirty-year career as an expert witness on capital crimes, I have interacted with many former gang members who were being tried for their crimes.

One day, my colleague and I visited the Dixon Correctional Center in Dixon, Illinois, about an hour and a half from Chicago and three hours from my home. I met Russell at the prison. After being properly searched, we were escorted into the visiting room to see Rico Johnson. Having already met other leaders of major gangs, I was able to make some comparisons. Rico came into the visiting room, sat down, and seemed very much at ease. He apparently had already received some information about me; he sized me up as we casually began our conversation. Nothing about this visit would lead me to think he was a person of stature or the leader of one of the major gangs in the United States.

As in our subsequent meetings, Rico was very polite, and in no way did he attempt to show me how important a figure he was. Actually, there was one exception in this regard. I was visiting with him one day when he pointed out a new inmate. He said that this particular man, a Vice Lord from the streets, had failed to show him respect when he arrived at the prison. Consequently, it was necessary for Rico to show him the error of his ways. After this brief aside, we went on to discuss other matters.

In addition to several meetings at the prison, Rico and I had other contacts over a period of several years. On two occasions, through the University of Northern Iowa phone hookup, he answered questions posed by members of one of my biggest youth-gang classes. Again, he was natural and eager to be help the students understand the impact of gangs on young people around the country. I also appeared on Rico's behalf at several parole hearings. Most of these took place at the Dixon Correctional Center.

The Illinois Department of Corrections at the time instituted a policy forbidding gang activity in the prison; violating this policy would result in being placed in disciplinary segregation or even sent to another facility. Realizing the potential consequences of my relationship with Rico, I had no further communication with him for several years. I did, though, indicate that when he was released from prison, I wanted to do his biography.

After his release in the fall of 2012, I received notice that he was out. I made two trips to Chicago to see him that fall, and we began the process of drafting an outline and interviewing individuals for this biography. Algie Crivens conducted a three-hour videotaped interview with Rico.

I have written a number of biographies of prominent individuals who have made significant contributions to their professions, including a warden of a maximum-security prison for men, the former director of the Federal Bureau of Prisons, and a professor of philosophy at a major Ivy League institution. I also did a study of juvenile correctional institutions that featured the views of two superintendents of juvenile facilities. Unlike those prior works, this biography starts from a negative foundation, looking first at the subject's childhood and youth, and then continues through stages of illegal activities and imprisonment until his reformation and release years later.

Willie Rico Johnson, now known as Rahim Johnson or Rahim Justice El, comes from a far different background than the subjects of my other biographies, and he has made a substantial impact on very different groups. However, like the other individuals I have written about, he hoped to make a difference in the world, and in that, he has succeeded. Granted, he has committed crimes and been in prison a major part of his years, but his life is still deserving of attention because of his determination to bring good from what once was anything but good. It is my great honor to be part of this project.

Acknowledgments

In the process of writing this biography over the past four years, I have received considerable help and much kindness from many people. First of all, Rico Johnson has done everything possible to be helpful, including spending hours being interviewed, setting up interviews, and providing transportation when I visited him in Chicago. I even had a bodyguard on my last trip there. I asked him what would happen if I should be taken out. He informed me that it would be curtains for him as well (he put it in a much more graphic way).

Special thanks to Algie Crivens for his willingness to tape three hours of interviews with Rico. In addition to doing an extremely professional job, he also kept the interviews going with his lively and pertinent questions. I am grateful too for all those willing to be interviewed. L. J. Musayah was particularly help for his assistance at the end of the project.

Special thanks also go to Dr. Nehemiah Russell, who has been my mentor with Chicago gangs since the 1990s. He was the one who initially introduced me to Minister Rico in an Illinois prison, and in the intervening years, he has kindly and perceptively answered my questions concerning this project. I am grateful as well to Alice Heiserman, my agent, who has been with me on four book projects. Finally, I acknowledge the support of my wife, Linda. She has been a blessing, and each day I tell her how thankful I am to have her in my life.

1

Overview of the Vice Lords

This is the biography of one of the leaders of the Conservative Vice Lords. To understand the background and development of this Chicago gang, I will discuss its origins in the 1950s and early 1960s; its community outreach programs; its most influential leaders, including David Dawley and the role he played; and its branches on the street.

Origins of the Vice Lords

The Vice Lords comprise the second-largest gang in Chicago, perhaps numbering around 10,000 in 2018. Its roots date back to the early 1950s on the west side of Chicago. It was known then as an athletic club called the 14th Street Clovers. When members of the crew got into trouble, they found themselves confined at the St. Charles Reformatory for Boys.

In 1958, seven of these African American youths from the area of North Lawndale formed a new gang called the Vice Lords. At first, the name was Conservative Lords; then it became Imperial Vice Lords, but Edward Pepilow "Pep" Perry, their leader, did not like the "Imperial" part because the Imperials had rejected him, so "Conservative" was used instead. "Vice" was chosen when another of the gang's founders, Leonard "Cal" Calloway, looked up the term in the dictionary and found one meaning was "having a tight hold." One of the goals of the Vice Lords was to unite North side, West side, and South side Lawndale boys.[1]

Early members of the Vice Lords were gradually released from the custody of the St. Charles Reformatory; they returned to the Lawndale community and subsequently recruited other African American youths to join their ranks. As a result of their effective recruitment, the Vice Lords grew quickly, and members were constantly involved in conflicts with other neighborhood gangs. With a reputation for violence and the use of extortion tactics, the Vice Lords were feared throughout the Lawndale community.

Bobby Gore, their legendary leader, adds what made the Vice Lords so popular in the community:

> And when they were released from St. Charles, they brought the gang to the street. As a result of that, they started recruiting. People were out in the street, no identity, they felt unloved, they were in essence, nobody. Everybody wants to be recognized as somebody, like Reverend Jesse Jackson [says]. I am somebody. I may be poor. I may be whatever it is, but I am somebody. I'm a human being. I want no less nor no more than anybody else has or what I can accomplish in terms of my own skills, in terms in trying to build what is a business or learning how to be a plumber or whatever. I want to do the same things everybody else wants to do. And that is to earn enough money to care for my family, if, in fact, I have a family or when I get a family. Through the years 1958 to roughly 1961, 1962, we started off like all the rest of the gangs.[2]

Thus, according to Gore, a group of young men at St. Charles in 1958 joined together for survival. They soon discovered that there was power and influence in their numbers, including institutional privileges such as getting extra food. Once they returned to the community, this group of boys, who called themselves the

1. Gore, "Conservative Vice Lords of the 1960s."
2. Ibid.

Vice Lords, began to annex other gangs to their group. Members in this emerging West side gang expanded their range of criminal activities.

By 1964, the Vice Lords were a main target for law enforcement. Their fights with other races escalated due to their serious and ongoing illegal activities, including robberies, thefts, batteries, assaults, intimidation, and extortion. In an attempt to soften their image and change the public's perception of their organization, they tacked "Conservative" onto the front of their name. The Conservative Vice Lords faction of the Vice Lords became the foundation for the entire Vice Lords Nation, or VLN. The Conservative Vice Lords also adopted new identifiers, such as the top hats, gloves, and canes they sported, to communicate their status as a more socialized group. They also tried to promote themselves as a community outreach organization and petition for a new chapter under the name Conservative Vice Lords Corporation, Incorporated (CVL, Inc.).[3]

Organizational Structure

The Vice Lords abide by twenty-one "supreme constitutional laws," among them "death before dishonor," "code of silence," "business before pleasure," and "take no shorts." In addition, the gang has commandments. Their regular meetings, usually held every week, are called goals and golden gatherings. When they adopted Islam in the 1970s, two concepts were actively embraced—the Al-Fatiha and Holy Divine, which in fact is a prayer and oath for gang members.[4]

The gang members wear black (signifying race) and gold (wealth). They sometimes have worn earrings and black capes emblazoned with the words *Vice Lords* in gold. They tend to greet

---

3. Dawley, *Nation of Lords*, 29.
4 Ibid.

each other with the slogans "All is well" and "Almighty." They refer to one another as "lord," "family," or "Joe."[5]

Organizational Leadership of the Vice Lords

The organizational leadership is as follows:

Supreme Chief—King of Kings

Prince of the Nation

Minister of Justice

Almighty Minister

Kings of the Nation

Universal Elites

Ambassadors

Minister of Command

Precinct Elites

Lieutenants

Minister of Literature

Symbols and Emblems

Vice Lord street gangs use a variety of gang graffiti symbols or emblems, to identify themselves and their gang "turf" including:

- A hat cocked to the left side. (Left represents the Peoples Nation alliance and cocking to the right represents the Folks Nation alliance.)
- Rabbit wearing a bow tie.
- Martini glass.
- A glove.
- Top hat.

5. Conservative Vice Lords, http://chicagogangs.org/index.php?pr=CVL.

- Cane.

- Five-point star—The five points represent (clockwise from top): Love, Truth, Peace, Freedom, and Justice.

- Crescent moon.

- Pitchfork pointing down—The pitchfork is a symbol of the Folk Nation.

- Broken heart with wings—A heart with wings is a symbol of the Gangster Disciples; breaking it is a sign of disrespect.

- Like the Black P. Stones, the Vice Lords often utilize pseudo-Islamic ideology and symbolism in their gang motifs.

- Pyramid with an eye above it.

- A six-point star broken in half to disrespect Folk Nation.[6]

Community Outreach Programs

In the late 1960s the Vice Lords and the Blackstone Rangers, two of Chicago's supergangs, became involved in programs of community outreach. Their social action involvement began in the summer of 1967 when the Vice Lords' leaders attended meetings at Western Electric and Sears and Roebuck. Operation Bootstrap, which resulted from these meetings, formed committees for education; recreation; and law, order, and justice. A grant from the Rockefeller Foundation in February 1967 enabled the Vice Lords to fund a host of economic and social ventures. Gang members also worked with Jesse Jackson on Operation Breadbasket and, in the summer of 1969, joined with the Coalition for United Community Action to protest the lack of African American employees on construction sites in African American neighborhoods.[7] See chapter 3 for a lengthier discussion of these community outreach programs.

---

6. Ibid.
7. Gore, "Tell Them What We Did!"

The supergangs in Chicago also became involved in political activism when they joined together to work against the reelection of Mayor Richard Daley and his Democratic machine. This activism brought added strain to their relationship with the Democratic Party organization. With Daley's reelection, gangs in Chicago began to experience what they perceived as harassment from the police. As soon as he began his new term, Daley announced a crackdown on gang violence, and State's Attorney Edward Hanrahan followed his lead by appraising the gang situation as the most serious crime problem in Chicago. The courts complied with this crackdown by increasing dramatically the number of gang members sent to prison in Illinois.

Leaders of the Conservative Vice Lords

At least four gang members have been instrumental in the development of the Vice Lords: Pep Perry, Bobby Gore, Willie Lloyd, and Rico Johnson. [8]

Edward Pepilow "Pep" Perry: After the founding of the Vice Lords at St. Charles Reformatory in the late 1950s, Pep Perry and Alfonso Alford emerged as leaders. David Dawley's *Nation of Lords* is particularly useful in understanding the role Pep Perry played in the development of the Vice Lords. [9]

According to Dawley, Pepilow had actually thought of forming a new gang before he was sent to St. Charles. He had attempted to join the Imperials but was not accepted. With a couple of other guys, he started a group called the Phantom Burglars. It was at that time he was sent to St. Charles, where he quickly established himself as a leader. Impressively built (around 6 foot 1 inches and 190 pounds), fast on his feet, and quick with his hands, Pep played football, basketball, and baseball, and was a good boxer.

As new guys came into the institution, Pep checked them out. When Leonard Calloway arrived at the facility, Pep realized

8. Dawley, *Nation of Lords*, 29.
9 Ibid.

he now had someone to help him get a club or gang organized, so he arranged to have Leonard assigned to the same cottage where he was housed. The original seven Vice Lords all had good jobs in the institution, which made it possible for them to control what was happening at St. Charles.

When the club started, the members had different ideas about what the Vice Lords would be. Maurice Miller expected that the club would be focused on social activities. Calloway anticipated that they were going to stay tight with the Imperials but just continue to have a club of their own. But Pep was the leader, and he had no intention of remaining close to the Imperials.

By the time of their release in 1961, Pep had acquired a reputation for taking care of those in his gang. He found girls to keep his fellas happy, he got them discount clothes because his girlfriend owned a clothing store, and he supplied money to his lieutenants and others down the chain of command. Pep always had $200 or $300 in his pocket, which he was willing to share.[10]

Pep was acknowledged as a good leader, for he was tough, violent, and smart. But in 1964, when he was twenty-one, Pep began spending more time with his family. Alfonso Alford gradually took over leadership of the Vice Lords. Before long, Pep left Chicago and went to Dartmouth University as part of the innovative Foundation Years Programs;[11] he was one of only a few African Americans at this Ivy League school. The CVL later sponsored a scholarship program for African American students to attend Dartmouth.

Unlike some of the other Vice Lords, Pep did not succeed at Dartmouth. He dropped out and returned to the Chicago streets, where was initially welcomed but later rejected by the Vice Lords. He also resumed the use of hard drugs. He was shot and died an early death.

10. Ibid.

11. The Foundation Year Program is a one-year introductory course to a full multi-year degree curriculum offered by many universities. Many of these programs are intended for those would not be in a degree program.

Bobby Gore: Bobby Fred Gore was the first in command—the ultimate elite—with the Vice Lords from the 1970s until his death in the spring of 2013. His given name was Fred Douglas Gore, but early on, his older sister, in an attempt to call him "baby," ended up calling him "Bobby," which is how that name got attached to Fred. Bobby was born in Cook County Hospital on May 13, 1936. He had two sisters; his father worked at the Chicago stockyards for thirty years, and his mother worked at home.

Bobby dropped out of high school in his senior year to help his parents financially. He joined the Clovers, since they were hanging out in his Lawndale neighborhood. The group was basically a social athletic club, and Bobby joined their baseball team. When Pep and others formed the Conservative Vice Lords after they got out of St. Charles, Bobby joined their gang. He would be a Vice Lord for the remainder of his life.

He was convicted of murder in the 1960s and spent eleven years and three months in prison before being released in 1979. He earned a general equivalency diploma (GED) and two bachelor's degrees while incarcerated. He spent the rest of his life attempting to receive a pardon for what he considered to be his wrongful conviction. (His case will be discussed in further detail in chapter 3.) Upon his release in 1979, he resisted involvement in the CVL because he disagreed with the gang's violence and drug dealing. Gore believed that such activities destroyed the community and undermined the values for which it stood. He worked as a counselor with the Safer Foundation for more than twenty years before his retirement, helping parolees recently released from prison find employment. He was a frequent speaker at colleges and in various community settings.

Here is one statement that Gore made on gangs:

> The gangs get the people that the parents don't have time for. The gang gets the high school dropout. The gangs get the people who are comin' out of jails. The gangs get all the stickup men, the dope addicts. As far as the system is concerned, the gangs are constructed of nothing but what the system cannot use, and they class us as garbage.

Any time a youngster gets with anything that has a gang label, they are just lost people. There is no hope. What we're trying to prove is that there is some good, and a lot of talent is going to waste right here with what the system says is no good. Our first priority is to show that we do have enough sense to do something.[12]

To the end of his days, Bobby Gore was committed to doing what he could to help the Vice Lords improve themselves through education, enhance their community through positive outreach programs, and better the lives of their families through jobs.

Willie Lloyd: As a teenager growing up on Chicago's West side in the 1960s, Willie Lloyd joined the Unknown Vice Lords, a faction based along 16th Street in the Lawndale neighborhood. In an interview I conducted with him, he spoke of how he was first attracted to the Vice Lords:

I grew up on the streets of Chicago. When I was growing up, the Lords had a big impact on me. I never saw it as a gang, but a cohesive and unified principle on which a person could organize his life. Even as a kid of nine, I was intrigued by the Vice Lords when I first saw them outside of the Central Park Theater. It was the first time I have ever witnessed so many black people moving so harmoniously together. They were motored by the same sense of purpose, and they all had similar dress and insignia. There were over a hundred guys, all in black, with capes and umbrellas. To my young eyes, it was the most beautiful expression I had ever seen. They all seemed so fearless, so proud, so much in control of their lives. Though I didn't know one of them at the time, I fell in love with all of them. In retrospect, I made up my mind the very first time I saw the Vice Lords to be a Vice Lord. [13]

Lloyd soon became the faction's leader and recruited thousands of followers. Eventually, he proclaimed himself "King of Kings" and stated that he was the leader of the entire Vice Lord Nation. However, his tenure was interrupted by a prison term after

12 Interview with Bobby Gore in February, 2013.

13. Interviewed in 1982 at the Iowa State Penitentiary at Fort Madison.

he was sentenced for his part in the murder of a police officer in Iowa.[14]

Lloyd continued to lead the gang on the outside through fellow inmates and prison employees affiliated with the organization. While incarcerated, he wrote *The Amalgamated Order of Lordism*, a sixty-one–page manifesto on the Vice Lord command structure in the prisons and on the streets. He was incarcerated from 1971 until his release on parole in 1986, then was back in prison a year later on a weapons conviction until another parole was granted in 1992. When he left prison then, he was picked up by fellow gang members who had a mink coat for him to wear, and he was driven from prison in a convoy of five limousines.[15]

Later in 1992, he participated in a protracted gang war over control of the Vice Lord Nation, involving kidnapping and the murder of rival members' children. Law enforcement intensified its efforts to remove Lloyd from the streets, and from 1994 to 2001, he was again incarcerated for weapons violations.[16]

During Lloyd's quarter century as the Unknown Vice Lords' leader, the gang's drug deals, extortion, and other crimes reportedly led to thousands of homicides. In 1996, police were said to have linked every murder committed in Chicago's 15th District to orders issued by Lloyd. He supposedly quit the Vice Lords after his release from prison and went on to become an outspoken critic of gang life.[17] Lloyd attempted to earn a living as a gang mediator, and he became affiliated with a nonprofit organization as well as DePaul University, where, for a brief period, he was a guest lecturer; his work there was controversial, in part due to a "field trip" Lloyd had scheduled for his students on the West side, which placed his students in some risk.[18]

In August 2003, Lloyd was shot four times while in Chicago's Garfield Park. This was the third assassination attempt on his life,

14. "Willie Lloyd—Drug Dealer."
15. Ibid.
16. Ibid.
17. Ibid.
18. Ibid.

and it left him temporarily paralyzed from the neck down. Rumors persisted that Lloyd still wanted to collect a "tax" from the Vice Lords as its leader, even though he had supposedly left gang life. He gave interviews stating that he believed his attackers included some of his former gang members. In 2014, at the age of sixty-four, Willie Lloyd was taking his dogs for a walk when he was shot to death.[19]

I might add a personal note here. Having interviewed "Chief Willie" at the Iowa State Penitentiary in 1982, I was receptive to continuing our conversations when he got out of prison. However, Rico warned me to stay away from Lloyd because there was a hit out on him; if I was present during the hit, he explained, I could be taken out too. I followed Rico's advice and had no more contact with Lloyd.

Willie Rico Johnson: Willie Rico Johnson has gone by a number of names during his life—Little Rico when he was an adolescent and Minister Rico during his early prison years. Sometimes he was called "the ol' man" while in prison, and he finally legally changed his name to Rahim Justice El on September 30, 1992.

From his boyhood on, Rico dreamed of becoming head of the Vice Lords. In front of him was Pep Perry, and after Pep left to attend Dartmouth College in the early 1960s, he was replaced as leader by Alfonso Alford. By 1970, however, Pep was dead and Alfonso was paralyzed, both victims of gang violence. Bobby Gore became the spokesperson for the Vice Lords, but he was convicted of committing a murder and sent to prison for twenty-five to forty years; he served eleven years and three months before being released. Bobby emphasized education while he was in prison, and from the time of his release until his death in 2013, he continued, as the Vice Lord Supreme Elite, to urge the gang's members to stay away from drugs and crime and to get jobs. In Illinois prisons meanwhile, Samuel "Mahdi" Smith rose in the leadership ranks, followed by Minister of Justice Rico Johnson. Smith was killed on November 8, 1993.

19. Ibid.

This biography tells the story of Rico's rise to become head of the largest branch of the Vice Lord Nation, the Conservative Vice Lords. Since his release from prison in August 2012, he has been able to function as a gang chief; actually, this biography suggests he has been the godfather of the Vice Lord Nation. In 2013, he declared a truce with the leaders of the other branches of the Vice Lords. Unlike Willie Lloyd, the chief of the Unknown Vice Lords who survived several assassination attempts before he was killed, Minister Rico was not physically threatened.

David Dawley: David Dawley arrived in Chicago in the summer of 1967. Determined to get at the roots of poverty, he sought out the Conservative Vice Lords, which was known as the most violent gang in the city. He was accepted into their ranks and ended up staying in the gang for two years.[20] He became a guiding voice and presence within the Vice Lords and helped convert the group from a street-hustling gang to a community-based organization. He worked with them to clean up the Lawndale neighborhood, as they started businesses and campaigned for the rights of the poor. In addition, Dawley was instrumental in the Vice Lords' effort to obtain grants for their community projects. Upon leaving Chicago, he wrote *Nation of Lords: The Autobiography of the Vice Lords,* which contains a great deal of interview data from the gang members, especially in the 1960s and 1970s.

Divisions of the Vice Lords

In the 1960s, there were about twenty-six branches of Vice Lords, but today, there are fewer than half that number. Rico claimed that it was drugs that resulted in this division. Along with the Conservative Vice Lords, the current branches include:

- Cicero Insane Vice Lords
- Imperial Insane Vice Lords
- Mafia Insane Vice Lords

20. Dawley, *Nation of Lords.*

- Traveling Vice Lords
- Renegade Vice Lords
- Unknown Vice Lords
- Four Corners Hustlers

In this overview of the Vice Lord Nation, it becomes clear that the culture of the inner city is one of survival. For those who do not live it, it is difficult to understand life on the streets.

For those who do live it, victimization, violence at the drop of a hat, selling and using drugs, and joining and staying with the gang all make sense as a way of life.

2

Mommy's Little Man

On February 23, 1945, Willie Johnson was born in Chicago. He had seven sisters and one younger brother; he was the fifth child. His mother, a native of Mississippi, was a nurse. His father, who was born in Chicago, remained in the home for only a few years. As a result, Rico's mother was forced to raise her nine children as a single parent.

Rico's Early Years

Rico never met his grandparents, who lived in Mississippi, but his mother used to tell him what her father would do to him if he were around. In a recent interview, Rico reflected on how his grandfather might have brought discipline to his life:

> He might have been able to stop me from some of the silly things I was doing. I was nine or ten years old, sneaking out of my mother's house and breaking into parking meters. I was stealing so much that I had $300 or $400 in my pocket every day. . . . [My mother knew that] I was a problem child.

Asked whether he ever got a "whooping," he responded:

Yeah, I got whoopings, but not the kind of whoopings that normal kids would get, you know. My mother would try to whoop me and I'd leave. I'd go to my auntie's. My auntie would lie to her, tell her I ain't there, and she would just stick up for me. My mother said "When you see him, tell him come on home, I got something for him." She meant that she was gonna whoop me if I came home, so I would stay at my auntie's and go to school from her house. I learned to ride the bus because I was from the streets.

Rico lived in a gray brick, two-story house. Across the street was a horse barn, and down the street was a vacant lot where semitrucks were parked. "On the other side of the street were just two or three buildings where people lived. On the corner of the street was a store. There might have been maybe ten families in the whole community on that block. Only about ten buildings on that block that was livable, the rest of it was merchandise or wholesale properties."

The makeup of the neighborhood when Rico was growing up was African American. At the time, the area was composed of "working families who had a good sense of community. It was mostly two-family households." Rico went on: "I've always had a good relationship with other kids' parents because I knew how to appeal to people, you know. I knew how to 'yes ma'am and no ma'am,' act that innocent role where I was the devil in disguise, so I had a very good relationship with other kids' parents."

When asked about basketball, football, or baseball, Rico responded, "I didn't have none of that; none of that interested me. The only thing that interested me was fighting, learning how to fight." He noted that the other kids played basketball, baseball, and football, but he was never drawn to those team sports.

Rico recalled one harrowing story from his early days:

I was sitting on the curb one night, and my mother was sitting on the porch, and one of the horses got out of the barn that was across the street from us. This horse was [rearing] up, and I was sitting on the curb, and I did not recognize it. If my mother had not called me, he probably would have stomped my brains out. She called me and told me: "Junior, get off that curb." And I'm mad, 'cause I'm thinking she's telling me to come in, but she's telling me to get my ass from under that horse. When I raised up to run, the horse was up like this here [both arms held overhead] ready to come down. I ran across the street and ran straight to my momma. That was a time of fear, then. Yeah, that was some fear I had.

Rico was a ghetto child. His father was gone more than he was present, and his mother struggled to support her nine children; money was always an issue. Besides the scarcity of money, there were many other signs of ghetto life in young Rico's world. The basement apartment they lived in for eight or ten years had three bedrooms, one bathroom, and a living room area. The large family had to make do in this small living space: the idea of seven daughters using one bathroom, especially when they got ready for school, is hard to contemplate. Another aspect of ghetto life was the prevalence of crime in the neighborhood. And there was a constant problem with the lack of services for those who lived in these apartments. Ghetto dwellers never rose too far above the poverty line. It is hardly surprising that so many decided to withdraw into alcohol and drugs. And before long, crack cocaine came to the streets of Chicago.

Rico mentioned that his family never went on vacations because they could not afford them. Everyday survival was a perennial issue for them. It was challenging enough for his mother to put food on the table, pay the heating bill, provide medical care, and occasional spend a little extra on her many children. Trips and special outings simply were not financially feasible.

Rico's favorite place to go to when he was a kid was the Riverview Amusement Park. He recalled, "It had all sorts of rides, and it was located on Western and Belmont in the city of Chicago. You could take the railroad bus to Western, and Western all the way out to Belmont. You could ride fast wheels, mobile cars, the hurdles, all of the old crazy fast rides and stuff. You see all kinds of displays in the areas. It's been so long I can't remember all the things that the Riverview had, but it was a very fun place to go." Rico said that many guys would ride to the park together, and to have a little more money to spend there, they would "snatch a pocketbook or something, to get a few extra dollars."

His mother rarely knew where he was, for even though the children had a curfew, Rico never followed it. His mother usually worked from three in the afternoon to midnight, which left him with precious little supervision. Without controls and discipline, he literally went wherever he wanted and did whatever he wanted, and at least in the early years, he did not need to consider the consequences of his behaviors.

Rico mentioned a couple of fears he had while growing up, both of which were related to ghetto life: (1) he was afraid of growing up and getting lost, and (2) he was afraid of being taken away without being able to survive. These fears clearly had to do with losing control of his life, and he intended to thwart such feelings by always being in control. He would be a dutiful son at home and do what he could to provide for his family. But at the same time, he would bully other kids his age in his neighborhood and exert leadership in the emerging Vice Lords organization. At this time, he was in the "peewee" level of the gang's structure, but it would not be long before he was in the "intermediate" and then the "senior" ranks (the adult version of the Vice Lords). Significantly, at the age of sixteen he already was planning to be a leader of the Vice Lords.

Given his fears of losing control, it is a sad irony that he ended up spending forty-one years of his life in prison. Being incarcerated is the ultimate loss of control, as others totally dictate what you are expected to do—what time you get up, when you go to breakfast, what you do throughout the day and in the evening, and what time you go to bed. Being confined to prison is like being treated as a child, and it is remarkable that Rico was able to handle his incarceration as well as he did, as long as he did, and with the obstacles he had to surmount.

Rico observed that "being raised in a family with no male structure is like a lion being turned loose in a pit with nothing to eat, and an instinct to survive." He added: "I think my fears came from the thoughts of my mother having to do without, my sisters having to be subjugated to men in order to survive, so my fears were being taken away from my mother and sisters without me being able to provide for them."

In his younger years, Rico was small and lean, and he would remain slim until his late fifties. But in his final years in prison, he started to gain weight; today, he weighs more than 250 pounds, which is more than twice what he did as a youth. Regardless of his weight, however, Rico's presence is such that he commands respect. When he comes into a room, he is noticed. Part of the respect that he has always garnered stems from his ability to box and use his hands.

Even as a young boy, he was more than able to hold his own. From about eight years of age, he became part of a small gang called the Jew-Town Boys.

> There was an older guy involved with us; his name was George, and he taught us everything we know. We were known as "the Jews-boys down in Jew-town," because all of the Jews in the city of Chicago sold merchandise in Jew-town. . . . This gang was only made up of the tough guys in the neighborhood. Members of the gang went back and forth in each other's homes. When they got a little older, younger members of the gang went to the Audy Detention Facility, while the two older members, Bony and Duke, headed to the county jail. Bony taught the younger members how to steal, including robbing people, breaking into houses, clothing stores, and so forth.

The Family

Rico's mother became his role model. But for her part, it was not long before she recognized that her son could be a problem. He always wanted his way. His temper was sometimes a problem. And anytime he felt like doing something, he did it without regard for the consequences. Not surprisingly, school did not go well for him, and he had some difficulty getting along with his teachers. Rico only went to the seventh grade in school, although he would do well in college-level work later in life.

Rico's mother was a good Christian woman, a faithful Baptist, and she went to church every Sunday. But early in his life, Rico showed little interest in religion. It was not until his prison years that he converted to Islam. He has been faithful to the beliefs and practices of that religion ever since.

His father eventually left the family home and did not return. His mother divorced him, and she never remarried. So even though Rico was her fifth child, he was the oldest of her two sons and thus became the surrogate father for the family. His siblings looked up to him, and before long, his mother became dependent on his support.

Rico said that they had three meals every day. Breakfast was mostly cereal, eggs, and toast. Lunch would be a sandwich with some peanut butter. Dinner would be beans, cornbread, okra, black-eyed peas, or liver. He recalled: "My favorite meal as a child was liver and rice, fried corn, and smothered okra." He always thought his mother was the best cook around.

Rico saw himself as the one who had to help his mother and relieve her burdens. He felt it was his job to bring money to her so that she could pay the bills, buy clothing and groceries, and have a little money here and there as was necessary for such a large family. He elaborated on how he obtained this money: "I would go out and do unsavory things—robbing, stealing, and looting. I would do what I could to help my mother do what she had to do and be there for the kids. My father might as well have been dead because he was no help to us. I had to pick up the slack where I could. I'm not trying to make excuses for the crimes I was committing but I did what I had to because I was my mother's man of the house."

His mother had little choice but to accept the money he gave her, for it put food on the table, helped pay the light and heat bill, and enabled her to clothe her children. Like many mothers who have a houseful of kids and limited financial means, she was almost overwhelmed by the responsibilities she carried on her shoulders.

It was hard to turn this money down and thereby deprive her children. One of the fears of every ghetto mother is having the heat turned off in the winter because the bill has not been paid. And Rico and his family lived in Chicago, which is not known for gentle winters.

His mother did try to speak with Rico about possibilities that would keep him out of trouble, such as becoming a schoolteacher, professor, or doctor. She told him that she would pray for that. Rico stated, "She used to talk with me about her being a nurse, what she thought I could do or would do if I just gave myself to it. It was good talking, but it was not very productive."

She knew that there were risks involved in what Rico was doing to make money—she didn't want to think about it, but she knew. And she was all too aware of the potential consequences of his illegal activities. In the years that followed, as Rico became involved in serious crimes and spent several years in prison he felt that he had let his mother down, but in her own way, she herself understood that she had contributed to the problems in his life.

Rico's sisters were also dependent on the money that he brought home. He would leave cash in the house so that it was available to them when they needed a bicycle, a skirt or blouse, or something else. Around their apartment, there would always be shoeboxes full of parking meter money or South Water Market money available for their needs.

Rico's sisters also knew that he was the favorite child in the household. Supper would not begin until he arrived home. Whatever TV program he wanted is what the family watched. When Rico barked, so to speak, the sisters learned to jump. And though he helped provide for their financial needs, the sisters all knew that Rico got whatever he wanted and that it was unwise to oppose him. At times, they resented "the favorite one," but they knew it was wise to keep their feelings under the surface.

Rico had one brother, Quan, who was five or six years younger. Rico described him as a "very sensitive guy and very studious. I never wanted him to be like me, so whatever I was doing, I would not allow him to socialize with me because I wanted to keep him safe from that. So, all of his young life, he had no experience with the law. He never became involved in a criminal case until he was grown."

He did mention that, from time to time, he taught his brother how to fight. On a few occasions after he got out of jail or a detention center, Rico would hang out with his brother, showing him how to defend himself, how to attack, how not to attack, when to attack, and what to watch for in a fight, until Quan understood enough to defend himself.

Rico acknowledged that there was little love between his father and himself. But the man did show up on holidays.

> All the time, all the time. Every Christmas, every Thanksgiving he would come by. I recall one Thanksgiving he came back and he was drunk. I think I was about eight years old. He brought a couple of his friends by, and they tore my mother's house up, destroyed her Thanksgiving dinner. And at that time, I was so little I couldn't defend her, so I had to get between her and him by blocking the door. And he saw I wasn't going to move from the door, so he just started throwing shit at her, you know? And that was part of my development of wanting to get even with him over the years, so that's when I started learning how to fight.

Rico, who realized early on that his father was an alcoholic, described him as "a poor excuse for a man. I didn't know that then, but as I grew older and became a man, I was determined to get even with him."

When Rico was asked about the discipline in his childhood home, he responded: "There was no discipline. My mother tried to do the best she could with nine kids, and it wasn't enough for me." As a male child growing up, Rico said, what he needed was "structure; some form of a man's structure to give me guidance, to show me which way I was going, how to get to where I was going, and what to do once I got there. With my father leaving, I didn't have that, so I took what I knew to be the best structure I had and that was the streets."

I asked Rico what he wanted to be as a child—what his dream job was. He answered: "I didn't have a dream job as a child, because as a child I was two years old before I started seeing things that I did not like [and] even at that age, I became so bitter and angry that I wanted to develop myself to be able to protect those that I love." "So, you didn't want to be a fireman or policeman?" I questioned. "No, all my life I wanted to be a boxer. My wanting to be a fighter was because of what I had seen in real life, not on TV. It wasn't so much as to beat people up as it was to protect people, and that's why I learned it. I learned how to protect my mother."

Asked if he was ever bullied or intimidated in school, he replied, "No, never. I was never the one that was bullied. If any bullying went on, I did it." He concluded, "I knew I had a few young guys that believed in me and [would follow] me to hell and back, and that's where I took them."

Running the Streets

In truth, Rico was already on the streets at a very young age. As he put it, "I was running the streets long before I was my mother's man of the house and that is one of the reasons I started going the route that I did."

Even as a youngster, he understood how important reputation is on the streets. He knew that it was critical to become a respected member of his subculture and that his peers had to learn not to mess with him. In the development of his reputation, one begins to see the leadership qualities that Rico would demonstrate through the rest of his life.

For gang leaders such as Minister Rico, *respect* is an all-important word. If someone does not give you respect, this is sufficient grounds to dole out extreme punishment. But it is not terribly difficult to understand the premium placed on respect when one realizes that most gang members, both youths and adults, have been disrespected in so many ways from their earliest days. Perhaps they cannot gain respect from the stakeholders in the system, but they had better be given respect from fellow gang members. This is particularly true when it comes to high-ranking gang members.

As a ghetto child with free rein to roam his neighborhood, Rico very quickly learned the law of the streets. In his tough urban environment, violence was all around him. He was exposed to the law of the jungle in his neighborhood and throughout Chicago. In his culture, it was accepted behavior to do whatever was necessary to maintain your image or reputation. This meant that you could not let anyone mess with you. Weakness could well cause your undoing, so you learned, along with your peers, that violence was a prerequisite for making it in ghetto life. (Of course, another way to make it was to be smart enough to remain in school and stay out of trouble or harm's way. But that was not the path that Rico and most of his friends would choose.)

In a violent culture, involvement in criminal activities can and does begin at a tender age. Rico acknowledged that his first run-in with the juvenile justice system occurred when he was not even eight years of age. He had gotten angry with his mother, so he knocked out a window and threw a stick at a motorcycle, causing the driver to have an accident. Rico ended up being taken to the Audy Home, a detention center in Chicago for young children. About a month or two later, he was in trouble again because he was robbing drivers of their money and taking fruits, vegetables, and other food, which he distributed to the community. Upon being apprehended, he was again sent to the Audy Home, and this time, he spent six months there.

Rico said that he left home when he was fifteen or sixteen and always had grown women to live with, which probably helped lead him down the wrong road. In the next chapter, I will discuss how he became increasingly involved with crime and gangs in his adolescent years.

3

Little Rico—
A Terror in the Community

Willie Rico Johnson was not a large adolescent; in fact, he was small, weighing just 130 pounds or so. This is why he was called Little Rico. Johnnie Walton, Sr., who was a childhood friend of Rico's and has been an invaluable help to me in charting Rico's adolescent years and his years in prison, said that neighborhood kids fought a lot when they were growing up. He himself fought both with and against Rico.[1]

Walton reported that "all of us were Conservative Vice Lords, because we hadn't started to branch out and spread over the West side of Chicago, just yet, but it was coming and coming faster than any of us realized." He talked about Little Rico's reputation on the streets: "Now there were guys with what we called 'reps' [reputations] big and small who were a terror out there in the streets, and I personally to this very day believe that 'the little shorties,' were the baddest and roughest because we always had something to prove! And we all wanted to be as rough as was Little Rico! Talking about the ultimate juvenile delinquent! That was 'Little Rico Johnson.'"[2]

---

1. Letter from Johnnie Walton Sr. on December 24, 2001.
2. Ibid.

At one point, Walton heard Little Rico was involved in an armed robbery that went terribly wrong; on the streets, it was even reported that it ended up with a murder. "Most of us youngsters," Walton noted, "didn't want to seriously hurt anyone back then! [But] to go to St. Charles or Sheraton was a badge of honor when you got back to the streets, and Little Rico Johnson had a chest full of 'honor badges' back in those days. St. Charles and Sheridan were like his second home."[3] He added:

> In those places we learned how to box real good, and some of us could box better than most professionals today. Little Rico Johnson took to boxing like a fish taking to water! I guess in part because he had this little person complex! What I called a "Napoleon complex"! Plus, he was consciously aware that we Shorty Vice Lords were outnumbered most of the time, and he was looked up to at that time as being one of the Shorty leaders! So, us Shorty leaders had to learn how to fight extremely good, because the leaders were called out to fight for the entire group! So, we heard about little Rico at that time and in those days and most of us fought to be just as rough and tough as little Rico Johnson.[4]

Rico was earning his reputation on the streets. He had been in and out of the Audy Home and jail since he was eight or nine years old. He had spent time in St. Charles and Sheridan and had learned to be quite a boxer. Even though he was a lightweight, he was in superb shape and could take care of himself.

Getting into the System

By nine years of age, Rico had already been in and out of reform school. As he put it, "I was trying to be a man before my time. Having seven sisters and a brother, I had to help the family make ends meet [through criminal activities]. My mother couldn't support us all."

3. Ibid.
4. Ibid.

Before getting into the system, Rico hung around with a gang of youths, and they were influenced by an older boy called Bony. His guidance to Rico and other kids centered on how to take people's money and rob stores. "He taught us how to break into clothing stores," Rico said, "how to go through the roof, how to go through the walls, and all the ways to make money. Instead of going to school, this is the education I received."

Rico's experiences in correctional settings were prominent through most of his childhood. He started this education in the Audy Home, which, as mentioned earlier, was a detention facility in Chicago. Rico admitted that while he was at Audy, he "was in a lot of fights," and when he was asked why he got into so many fights, he said, "Guys talking too much, irritating me. I used to have a temper, and it didn't take much. Just rub me the wrong way, and I'll pop you in the mouth. You'll pop me in the mouth, and there it goes."

From the Audy Home, he "graduated" to St. Charles in 1957 and returned there again in 1962 and part of 1963. Rico described the effect St. Charles had on him: "I did not get into much trouble until I went to St. Charles. I was worse off than before I went in there. I learned nothing, other than how to be worse off in the streets. I came out a young boy with a man's mentality. I started doing manly things."

Educators and others who are concerned about juvenile behavior have often noted that reform schools are breeding grounds for increasingly bad behavior. The Office of Juvenile Justice and Delinquency Prevention discussed some of the scholarship on this issue.[5] D. S. Lipsey and J. H. Derzon note that for youth ages twelve to fourteen, "a key predictor variable for delinquency is the presence of antisocial peers."[6] According to Joan McCord and colleagues

> factors such as peer delinquent behavior, peer approval of delinquent behavior, attachment or allegiance to peers, time spent with peers, and peer pressure for

5. https://www.ncjrs.gov/html/ojjdp/jjjournal_2003_2/page3.html.
6. Ibid.

deviance have all been associated with adolescent anti-social behavior.[7]

In addition to being educated in new modes of criminality and deviant behavior, Rico actually learned several trades at St. Charles—photography, shoe repair, and printing. What studying these trades taught him was to be eager about learning. He decided that he wanted to be more than a hustler. "Later in life," he noted, "I would run into people who had an interest in me, and they have also steered me toward educating myself."

From St. Charles, he was sent to Sheridan Industrial School for Boys. There, he learned more about repairing shoes, but his great love was boxing. At Sheridan, an older adult who taught residents how to box took a special interest in Rico, and before long, the young man began to excel with his hands.

Jim Reed, a staff member at Sheridan, was looked upon as an old white man, but he could box. And he taught everyone who came to him how to box as well. Little Rico was one of his best pupils. In fact, he worked with him every day: Rico would leave after classes and head straight for the gym. He reflected on the process of learning to box with Reed: "We would rough-ball, beat the heavy bag, learn your pivots, learn how to throw punches, learn how to roll with punches, throw punches, side-step, slip and slide, bob and weave. He taught you everything you needed to know about the fight game. We would also run laps and lift weights. I was in superb shape. He also taught me discipline. He taught me how to know what you want and go at it. He taught me how to pursue something, and he gave me an instinct to herd it and control it." This experience prepared Rico to take care of himself when he returned to Chicago. He has always regarded his training in boxing to be a major factor in his life. He feels it taught him discipline, self-control, and how to summon courage when confronted with a crisis.

7. DeWitt Beall, *Lord Thing: A Chicago Street Gang Tries to Go Straight,* 1970 Documentary Recall the Doomed Reform of the Conservative Vice Lords. Chicago Reader, 2016. By L. R. Jones Jr. Jones http://www.chicagoreader.com/lord-thing-movie-dewitt-beall-documentary-film/Content?oid=144438887.

Eventually, the consequence of the criminal activities Rico was involved with outside the gym brought him to the attention of the juvenile justice system, thus beginning his parade through juvenile and, later, adult institutions in the state of Illinois. His life story exemplifies the tragic reality that once youths get into the justice system, they often are in and out of correctional institutions for the rest of their lives. Of course, these individuals are the lucky ones; the unlucky ones have already gone to the cemetery.

When Rico was coming of age, gangs were not using weapons, and drugs were only starting to appear on Chicago's streets. What gang members did was fight with their hands, and the instructions that Jim Reed gave to his young charges proved invaluable in this regard. Upon returning to the streets, Little Rico was even more of a force to reckon with than he had been before.

Becoming a Vice Lord

It was at St. Charles that Rico was exposed to a developing street gang known as the Vice Lords, which was then regarded as a social gang. As the years went on, the Vice Lords would have a great influence on his life. Rico commented on the development of this social gang:

> The Vice Lords started in 1957 with a social club called the Conservative Vice Lords. It was formed as a way to help protect our communities. Somehow, the head got too far from the tail and all hell broke loose. Drugs were not part of the operation when it first started out. When we first started out, it was a social group that protected the community which we came from. As drugs become more prominent, that affected very much the development of gangs.

Rico noted that he became involved with the Vice Lords at St. Charles in 1957 and talked about the early history of the gang: "We had a leader by the name of Eddie Perry. He was the founding creator of the Conservative Vice Lord Nation, and we called him 'Pepilow.' He was from the West side of Chicago, a place called the

Holy City, which [ran from] 16th and Kensett, all the way to 16th and Pulaski, from Roville to Cermak."

He went on to describe Perry:

> He was a broad guy, six feet one or so, and he was like a defender for everybody from the West side of Chicago. At St. Charles, they had the South side, the North side, the West side, and he was like a defender to the West side of Chicago. What he done was created the Vice Lords in the basement of Harlan/Hartman Cottage. We were created in order to go to our communities and protect these communities, because back then they had a whole lot of raping, burglary, and robberies, and other stuff in the communities. He was something of a community person, but we left the jail and came to the city. We did not take advantage of where he was leading us.

As mentioned earlier, Pepilow got a scholarship to Dartmouth, but after attending for a while, he became ill and returned home. He was never able to serve as a leader for the Vice Lords again. In 1962 and 1963, Bobby Gore began to exert leadership and set up programs in the gang. Rico was somewhat involved in these "social betterment" programs, but he was more into establishing his reputation in the gang and on the streets.

Rico believed his more important goal was to represent the Vice Lords—to defend and uphold his gang at all costs. He wanted to protect the gang, to destroy anything and anybody that raised arms against it, including other organizations such as the Egyptian Cobras, the Braves (which were also called the Hawks), and the Tommy Hawks. These organizations, according to Rico, were doing what they could to seize control of the community. He remarked, "We wanted to make sure the women were safe, their homes were safe, and everyone was safe until we could shut them down."

In these early years of development, there was an initiation process for everyone in the community who wanted to become a Vice Lord. It was no longer enough just to be willing to join the gang; now, one had to be initiated. The process involved a fight. Two dozen or more brothers (current gang members) were lined up in two rows facing each other, and one more brother stood at the end of the row. The prospective member had to fight his way down the length of the row to the end where the brother was standing. The theory was that if you were strong enough to get through these guys, you were strong enough to be a Vice Lord.

Rico added more details about the gang in those days:

> The Vice Lords were divided into the Midgets, the Juniors, the Pee Wees, and the Singers.
>
> We also had a group called the Vice Ladies. They would actually be sisters that we would use in the community to traffic our weapons, so that we would have necessary means when we go to war. The Vice Ladies were also responsible for starting programs in the community representative of the Vice Lords.
>
> What we had then in the mid- to late 1960s was two different groups. There was one that was committed to defending the Vice Lords against other gangs, but at the same time, while it was protecting the Holy City against rival gangs, it was seeking to expand the territory and influence of the Vice Lords throughout the West side.

It was this group and its emphasis on expansion that attracted Rico and spurred his commitment.

The other emphasis was on social outreach programs that were initiated and funded in the 1960s. Pep Perry and later Bobby Gore were committed to these programs. Gore, as previously discussed, was a strong source of leadership for the Vice Lords in the 1960s, and he wanted community outreach and educational programs for the gang's members. His leadership was somewhat sub rosa, which tends to obscure just how dominant he was in the Vice Lords during the 1960s. However, by the end of that decade, he was tried and convicted for a crime and given a long prison sentence.

Social Outreach Programs

An article in the Chicago Crime Scenes Project posed this provocative question: "Can a group of street gang members with long police records, high school dropouts for whom drunkenness and violence were the core of daily life, one day decide to found a community development organization and become successful businessmen?" The article continued: "Between 1967 and 1970, the Vice Lords, once the West side's most feared gang, attempted just this. Their surprising successes and ultimately crushing failure symbolized the cycle of ghetto idealism during that period. At their peak, the Lords owned and operated five businesses in the 3700 block of W. 16th Street alone, plus several others nearby."[8]

In 1964, the Vice Lords had twenty-eight "sets," or branches, controlling a particular block or two, and up to 10,000 members. They controlled the majority of the territory between Pulaski and Western Avenue and from Lake Street south to Ogden. By this point, some of the founding members were sixteen to eighteen years old and were mature men with families. They saw the destruction their activities had brought to the community and understood the attraction of power and money that would continue to draw disaffected juveniles into gang organizations.[9]

In July 1964, some of these "older" members were hanging around getting drunk on the corner of 16th and Lawndale when a younger Vice Lord approached them to propose a violent attack on a rival gang. Alfonso Alford suggested that rather than launching an attack, they should instead do something constructive by opening businesses in the neighborhood.

In many respects, this idea of the Vice Lords opening businesses did not seem to make a lot of sense: after all, they may have had control of the streets of North Lawndale, but they totally lacked business experience. Yet Perry, Calloway, Alford, Gore, and

8. http://chicagocrimescenes.blogspot.com/2009/07/conservative-vice-lords-inc.html.

9. Ibid.

others began looking for ways to use their street power to generate positive change.

Around this time, rioting broke out in Chicago after the police released a white man who had attacked and killed an African American male with a baseball bat. Vice Lord members were heavily involved in the rioting and looting that ensued. Media attention given to the impoverished area brought greater awareness among politicians and the police about the dire situation there. One organization, the Southern Christian Leadership Conference (SCLC), sought to bring peace to Lawndale. There also was mounting concern about how to reform the hardcore youths who participated in the rioting and would likely continue to make trouble.

On January 22, 1966, Martin Luther King, Jr. moved into 1550 Hamlin Avenue in Chicago. He specifically attempted to work with the major street gangs of the city, inviting the Blackstone Rangers, Gangster Disciples, and Vice Lords to a Soldier's Field rally. King reached out to the leaders of all these gangs in hopes of securing their cooperation. The Vice Lords seemed to be more receptive to this civil rights leader than the other Chicago gangs. Indeed, a number of Blackstone Rangers walked out of the rally when King made a critical comment about gangs.

West side businesses such as Carson Pirie Scott and Sears and Roebuck, which were afraid of the losses that would occur if rioting erupted, formed a group called Operation Bootstrap with the Vice Lords and two other West side gangs, the Roman Saints and the Cobras. The group held meetings through the summer of 1967 for the purpose of establishing constructive dialogue between business leaders and gang members. With the assistance of David Dawley, the Vice Lords incorporated as the nonprofit organization Conservative Vice Lords, Inc., in September 1967. They applied for and received a $15,000 grant from the Rockefeller Foundation. This was matched with an equal amount from Operation Bootstrap and was followed by $25,000 from the Ford Foundation, $36,000 from the Department of Labor, and $60,000 from W.

Clement Stone. Partnership with the Vice Lords was seen as a way to reach individuals who were desperately in need.[10]

With the assistance of business leaders and the new funding, the Conservative Vice Lords turned the north side of the 3700 block of West 16th, once composed mostly of dilapidated and abandoned buildings, into a thriving business and community center. Between the fall of 1967 and 1969, the following developments took place:

- Teen Town, an ice cream parlor that catered to youths, was opened.

- The African Lion, an Afrocentric clothing shop, was opened.

- The House of Lords—a recreation center for teens, with table tennis, jukeboxes, books, and card tables—was opened. Another was later opened at a second location.

- Art and Soul—a free, open-door facility for community members—was opened, providing a space where youths could paint and engage with art. This facility was opened in conjunction with the Museum of Contemporary Art, the University of Illinois–Circle Campus, and the Illinois Sesquicentennial Commission.

- Two Tastee Freeze franchises were also opened for the community.

- The Department of Labor funds were further used to start a management-training institute to develop business skills.

- An Avon-like cosmetics line called Simone, featuring color tones especially for African American women, was planned.

- The West Side Community Development Corporation was established, bringing the Conservative Vice Lords together with four other groups to form an economic coalition.

- The Management Training Institute offered a twenty-week program that taught black history; self-awareness; reading;

10. Ibid.

and business skills such as banking, business correspondence, and salesmanship.

- The Street Academy was opened for high school dropouts, offering a way for young people to catch up on their education without leaving the community.

- An organization named Partners was opened to improve the executive skills of Conservative Vice Lords leaders.[11]

During the summer of 1968, the Catholic School Board awarded CVL, Inc., one hundred neighborhood youth jobs for the purpose of cleaning and beautifying public areas. Furthermore, the gang organized a tenants' rights pressure group to assist neighborhood residents in negotiations with landlords. The Vice Lords, as well as other gangs, also worked with civil rights groups to demand more jobs for African Americans in Chicago's traditionally white labor unions. The Conservative Vice Lords was becoming not only a community organization but a major political force in Chicago as well.[12]

The future seemed promising for the Vice Lords, but a number of factors and developments eventually returned the group to its former status as a major street gang in Chicago.

First, with the exception of Dawley, all the Vice Lord leaders were high school dropouts. Establishing a successful business is difficult enough for anyone, and most new businesses fail. But the gang's lack of management skills made success even more unlikely.

Second, instead of locating businesses close to customers and where they would have visibility and be likely to make a profit, Conservative Vice Lords, Inc., continued to invest in a particular neighborhood. This protectionist approach, or "local self-sufficiency," actually stacked the economic deck against the long-term success of CVL, Inc.

Third, while the gang leaders took salaries between $10,000 to $15,000, the rank and file continued to live in poverty and wanted to rise in the gang hierarchy. This was aptly expressed in

11. Ibid.
12. Ibid.

October 1967 with the intergang warfare between the Vice Lords and the Cermak Boys over turf. The violence was widely covered in the media and provoked negative public reaction. Key events in the troubled years that followed were the shooting death of a five-year-old boy in July 1968, the shooting death of one of the original Vice Lords in front of Teen Town in May 1969, and the kidnapping off the streets of two women who were repeatedly raped inside the African Lion.

Fourth, Major Richard J. Daley and State's Attorney Edward Hanrahan declared a "war on gangs." Gang members claimed that Daley feared the Vice Lords and the concentration of black political power they were developing. As a result of this war on gangs, there was a dramatic rise in the number of gang members, especially those in leadership capacities, being sent to prison. Bobby Gore, who had served as the primary spokesperson for the Vice Lords, as previously noted, was arrested, convicted, and sent to prison where he was to serve eleven years.

Fifth, because the CVL were having trouble with the law, the money from the government and philanthropic organizations dried up. A major contributing factor was that Jeff Fort and other members of the Blackstone Rangers were imprisoned for misappropriating funds. Although no evidence exists that Conservative Vice Lords were doing anything similar, the whole notion of philanthropic organizations working with street gangs was irreversibly tarnished. The foundations that had once competed over which would give the most money to the CVL now moved on to more fashionable pursuits such as environmental causes and nuclear nonproliferation.

Sixth and finally, in 1969 the gang's grant writer, David Dawley, returned home to Massachusetts. This was a major destabilizing development for the Vice Lords because in addition to writing grants, Dawley was always available to give prudent counsel and guidance. He particularly had credibility with the leaders of the Vice Lords.

During 1970 and 1971, the gang's once-proud set of businesses gradually closed. And it was during the 1970s that the Vice

Lords returned to their past status as a violent street gang. Their dominance on the streets of Lawndale positioned them to serve as a major player in the rising cocaine and crack drug sales.

Rico during the 1960s

Rico had earned the stature of a war counselor in the Vice Lords. This meant that he had the power to set up, create, or stop wars. So, if the gang had a confrontation with some other organization, it would be Rico's decision whether the Vice Lords would fight that group. In those days, when a fight took place it was waged with hands, rather than with the weapons that would eventually be used in gang warfare. As Rico put it, "We would meet in the park or wherever, and we would throw down."

As Rico began his revolving-door existence with the Audy Home, jail, St. Charles, and Sheridan, he knew he was letting his mother down, and that genuinely bothered him. However, he did not know how to break the cycle. Furthermore, he did not want to break it because from the first time he was exposed to the Vice Lords, he saw gang leadership as his career path. Perhaps he would even become the leader of the Vice Lord Nation.

Then in 1966, he was charged with armed robbery. In his bench trial, which took place when he was twenty-one, he appeared before a judge who gave him the choice of enlisting in the armed services or going to jail. Rico knew a man named Fred Hamilton who had faced this same alternative a year before and had chosen the armed services; Fred was not in Vietnam for very long before he was sent home in a body bag.

Rico quickly decided that he was going to jail to avoid a similar fate; beyond that, he was not willing to fight another man's war. After spending a brief time in the Cook County Jail, he was sent to Joliet Correctional Center, which served as a reception center for the Illinois prison system. He was finally shipped off to the Illinois State Correctional Institution at Pontiac, which was known at the time as an extremely violent facility. A year later, he was released to the streets, ready to begin the adult phase of his life.

As the next chapter narrates, when Rico was sentenced to prison as an adult in 1970, things really began happening in his life. He was given a sentence of twenty-five to one hundred years for murder, and knew he had to eat or be eaten—he had to choose between becoming a beast or being a meal. He chose to become the beast.

4

Early Prison Years and Survival

The story continues. In 1966, Rico committed an armed robbery. He explained his crime by saying that he needed money. Then, he took money from the soda pop, ice cream, and bread trucks that drove through his neighborhood. "We'd rob them so hard and so much," he said, "that companies would pay us to leave them alone. So, we would leave them alone, and then when we wanted to get more money out of them, we would rob the truck drivers again." He was arrested and appeared in court, and as mentioned in the last chapter, the judge gave him a choice between serving in the armed forces and going to prison. He chose prison.

Orientation to the County Jail

Before entering the penitentiary, Rico had to go to the Cook County Jail in Chicago. It was his first experience in that jail. On the day he arrived, he was taken to the F1 tier and informed that he had to "throw down"—that is, to box someone the "barn boss" had chosen who was about his size. In his first fight, Rico made a good impression. Before he was sent on to Illinois Correctional Center at Pontiac, he became a barn boss himself.

His mother visited him behind bars, and Rico remembered that "it was sad because they would only allow you a fifteen-minute visit. It was like standing up in the cage, and you visit for fifteen minutes. She would leave, and you would come back to the tier." On all the visits from his mother while he was locked up, Rico would think, "Oh, how I have let her down, how sad she was when she left." He resolved to change when he got out, but somehow, that never seemed to happen. He added: "I didn't want to hurt her. And this hurt was what I saw in her during the visiting. I tried not to show that I was hurt by it. So, I went back to my house [jail cell] and had some sad moments. Once it blew over, I just came on out and did what I normally do, just danced around the tiers and stayed strong."

Rico remained in the county jail for eight months and shipped out in December 1966, heading first for the Diagnostic Center in Joliet and then the Illinois Correction Center in Pontiac. He described his orientation at Joliet: "They would strip you down naked, put oil on your body, under your arms, on your privates. They would shave your hair off, shave your mustache, and your sideburns. . . . They'd give you a shower afterwards, give you a pair of blue pants and blue shirts, and send you to a cell—where you would remain until you go through the diagnostic orientation." In the short time he was at Joliet, he continued to fight, but by then, he had established a the reputation and did not have to prove himself as he had before.

While locked up and out of circulation, Rico did not know what was going on at home. But he did receive letters from his family, including his mother, sisters, aunts, and cousins. He would usually tear up his mail once he read it because "it had so many soft points in it, that made you have feelings—something you didn't need to feel under the circumstances."

Shipped to Illinois Correctional Center at Pontiac

The authorities decided to send Rico to Pontiac. When he heard where he was going, he thought to himself, "I'm going to a hellhole."

He explained: "It was a place where you went to where you could either be the prey or be preyed upon. Being that you don't want to be the food on the table, you become the server at the table. You would give out food instead of being served as food."

At the penitentiary, he was first taken to a clothing room, where they gave him three pairs of pants, three shirts, a heavy coat, boots, a hat, and a cup. Then he was escorted to a cell house, where he was assigned to a cell. He stayed there until he was given a job.

After two months, his mother visited him, as did his older sister Deliath. Until her death, his mother continued to visit Rico throughout his years of incarceration, and so did Deliath. I attended a parole hearing in the 1990s where Deliath and I were Rico's spokespersons. Once it was over—and we anticipated Rico would be turned down for parole as he had been before—Deliath and I talked for a while. Rico at the time was incarcerated at Menard Correctional Center, a maximum-security prison in Chester, Illinois, that was about 350 miles from Chicago. Deliath informed me that the cancer she suffered from had spread. As a result, she said, this would probably be her last visit to her brother. I live 200 miles from Chicago and wanted to take her to see Rico one more time before she died, but sadly, that did not happen. Her cancer had progressed too far to permit her to travel.

Looking back on his mother's visits at Pontiac, Rico remembered that before she left, she would begin to cry, which made him feel "real bad, real bad." When I asked him if it made him feel bad enough to change, he replied that he knew he did not have the ability to change at that time. Besides, he thought he was doing the right thing—he justified his criminal behavior by saying it had always been necessary because it helped to feed his sisters, brother, and mother. When I asked how he was supporting them while in prison, he said he was selling reefers inside the joint and sending his money home.

Back in the 1960s, developments on the streets influenced the prisons and their populations. For instance, the Black Panthers, whose basic concern was the dignity of the black man, wielded significant influence inside prison walls. Their focus was on direct aggression against the system. Panthers were told that if they stood together, they would be strong, but if they were divided, they would be weak and easily torn down.

Rico clearly understood the various organizations that were running the prison. He described what was going on and how each group functioned. The Disciples, the Cobras, the Roman Saints, and of course the Vice Lords all had their leaders. He continued: "The leaders of these organizations did not always get along and sometimes spearheaded real violence. But at that time, leaders of organizations would come together and form like a family and be peace-like. And that peace would hold them together to attack the administration."

Rico was seen as a barn boss, the head inmate on a given tier. He was already seeking to become a leader in the Vice Lords, and his leadership skills were growing more and more apparent to his peers. He was aware at the time that the Conservative Vice Lords within the prison were in a different place than the CVLs on the outside. The locked-up Vice Lords were gangbanging and fighting various organizations for control of the prison, moving the gang in a negative direction. But "outside of prison," he said, "the Vice Lords were developing all kinds of programs, projects, and businesses. I knew that outside the prison, we were becoming positive. We had been chartered, and we were a legal organization in the city of Chicago."

Release and Return to Chicago

Upon his return to the community, Rico said, he initially felt good about what the Vice Lords were doing for the neighborhood. "But then," he continued "it started to develop in all kinds of chaos. The people who were donating money and giving us grants to sponsor these projects and programs started to play politics with us." The Vice Lords were receiving grants from DuPont, Rockefeller, Sears and Roebuck, Oscar Brown, and others major corporations. He explained: "What I mean is that we were accused of misappropriating government funds by using them in ways that were not intended, such as gang members [using] these funds for themselves rather than [for] intended programs."

The Blackstone Rangers and their leader, Jeff Fort, had also received government and private funding for their programs, and they too were accused of corruption. In fact, some Blackstone Rangers, including Fort, wound up in prison for misappropriating government funding. Because the Conservative Vice Lords had received more private funding than the Rangers, the government opted not to have their leaders sentenced to prison to the same degree as the Blackstone Rangers. Ultimately, though, both these gangs would find that their funding, private and government alike, was cut off.

Rico noted that the Martin Luther King movement had hit Chicago by then. He stated that when he was released from Pontiac and returned home, King was living on the west side of Chicago, in Hamblin, "which is what we call the holy city. We went marching with him to Cicero in 1968. I got a chance to shake his hand, walk with him, and talk to him." He added: "He was just trying to make us understand what nonviolence was all about. And as he was talking, I was standing right next to him with a .22 pistol in my back pocket."

"So, you didn't buy his philosophy of nonviolence?" I asked Rico. "No," he responded, "but I did buy into his beliefs that we, as a people, could do better in what we were doing. But at the same time, I was more impressed with the Black nationalist, Malcolm X. I believed in Malcolm X, more so than King. When they were throwing rocks and bricks at King and us in Cicero, King told us to stay nonviolent, accept being stoned and beaten up. And that was not what we were taught or brought up with."

Rico went on: "Malcolm came into the city about the same time that Martin Luther King did in 1967. We were urged to support him. A sixteen-year-old pregnant black girl was killed in the community, and we rioted in the city and tore the city up. Malcolm X was very instrumental in instructing the black man to direct violence toward the white man. He said something like you must use whatever means is necessary. We believed that for real."

Rico's mother's respected King and was glad that her son was supporting him. She thought or at least hoped that Rico was following in his footsteps. She also knew about her son's involvement with Malcolm X, but that she did not like that. As Rico put it, "She knew that he was a bold black, but she really didn't understand his essence."

Rico discussed Malcolm X and his organization at greater length. He said that the black nationalist shook his hand, ate and conversed with him and others, and sat in on meetings with him. Rico spoke of some lessons he learned from Malcolm: "Well, we learned that most of the lies that were about him were just what they were—lies. We were told that most of what he advocated was truth and not chaos and confusion. . . . Malcolm also taught me to respect myself and to learn more about black people." Rico started to study black history, and at the same time, he started to develop a hatred for white folks.

Rico mentioned that the Black Panther Fred Hampton was killed around then, and he said he had had a relationship with Hampton. "I grew up with Fred Hampton. He was born and raised in Maywood. I was a gang banger, and he was a black nationalist. But, we had a relationship with one another that kept us communicating with each other." One program the black nationalists had at this time, Feed the Children, impressed Rico a great deal.

He also pointed out a contrast between the Vice Lords and the Black Panthers: "They [the Panthers] were more into military thought patterns and we were more into street thought patterns. What the Panthers was representing was the development of a nation, while what we were representing was the development of the Vice Lords."

Even as he delved into the philosophy of Martin Luther King Jr. and Malcolm X, Rico continued to run the streets, building his reputation and committing crimes. By 1969, he was on the run for an armed robbery. He went back and forth between locations as he tried to avoid capture. Then on January 13, 1970, he committed a murder on the west side of Chicago. Rico left town that night, but an old buddy from his neighborhood identified him to the authorities, and he was apprehended. He was taken to jail to await the criminal justice process. He feared he would be spending the rest of his life in prison.

The Context Was Not Friendly to Gangs

As suggested in the previous chapter, once the street gangs became political Mayor Daley declared war on them. In the 1968 mayoral election, Rico had campaigned for Daley's opponent but to no avail. Daley won the election and went after the gangs. The police were instructed to harass gang members and arrest them for whatever reasons that could be—either legitimately or illegitimately—manufactured, and judges were expected to give gang members long prison sentences. Gang leaders especially were to come under the heavy hammer of justice.

However, long before the late 1960s and the period when Daley machine was getting tough on gangs, the Chicago police had a history of violent relationships with gang members. David Dawley told of one incident that reflected this relationship:

> I saw 'em have one [gang member] handcuffed with his hands behind him in the chair and they just beat him on the stomach with one of the backjacks . . . the kind they don't use any more, round and a lot of lead. I saw 'em use a rubber hose and then the officer whip you, you be bruised up but the first thing they say is you resisted arrest and you tried to attack them so they had to do this. But how can a man beat you if he is handcuffed and why does he have bruises now when he [had] no marks when he got in the squad car? And usually they don't take the handcuffs off until they take you in their station and kick your ass.[1]

Dawley went on to say that the black police officers were the ones who created most of the abuse; the white police apparently did not bother the gang youths. In those days, black and white officers did not ride in the same car; therefore, black police would

1. Dawley, *Nation of Lords.*

be the ones who answered the calls in black neighborhoods. The white police felt that blacks were only cutting up and shooting and killing their own people. In a way, as they saw it, the gang youths were doing them a favor.[2]

Once Daley declared war on the gangs, gang youths experienced the full wrath of both white and black officers. One example of police justice in Chicago was the situation Mickey Cogwell, leader of the Four Hustlers, faced after he was picked up by police. When he refused to disclose any information, he was taken to a pier on Lake Superior, hung upside down, and informed that either he would talk or he would be dropped into the lake. Cogwell could not swim and was terrified of water. In what amounted to torture, he was willing to talk.

A more egregious example of Chicago court justice at the time was the trial of Fred D. "Bobby" Gore. Criminal Court Judge Robert J. Downing sentenced Gore, age thirty-three, for the murder of Thuman Williams, age twenty-three, outside the Tea Box Lounge, located at 3429 West Ogden. Three witnesses at the trial said they saw Gore go up to Williams, engage him in a fight, and then pull a gun and shoot him in the back. The witnesses said the gunman shot with his right hand, but Gore maintained during the trial that he was left-handed and thus was innocent.

His defense did not succeed. Gore was sentenced to twenty-five to forty years for the murder and also ordered to serve four to ten years on a charge of aggravated battery arising from this incident. The judge said that both sentences would run concurrently. Gore's attorney, Patrick Murphy, who went on to a distinguished career as a Chicago judge, challenged the conduct of Judge Downing and what was taking place in the trial time after time. After sentencing, Downing cited eleven incidents of "contumacious and unprofessional conduct" by Murphy during the trial and at the pretrial proceedings.

Rico experienced his own version of police or system justice in the murder case for which he was arrested, convicted, and sent to prison. The case involved one of his sisters, who was married

2. Ibid.

to a man who physically abused her on a regular basis. She had complained to Rico, and Rico and the husband had had words over this. Then one day, she called Rico and informed him that her husband had beaten her with a skillet, leaving her "messed up." Rico immediately went over to their house, and he and the husband were soon in a heated argument in the living room. The husband was on a couch, and he reached for a gun that was under the afghan he was sitting on. Rico beat him to the punch, fired his own gun, and killed the man. Though his attorney attempted to make a case for self-defense when the matter went to trial, Rico was convicted of murder and given a sentence of twenty-five to one hundred years in prison. On the face of it, it seems to have been another case entailing a gross miscarriage of justice.

Ironically, although Major Daley's get-tough strategy was working and he was getting gang members and their leaders off the streets, he was also creating problems for prison administrators because gang leaders were building their reputations in the joint as they went about the business of developing their organizations. In all of the Illinois prisons, the gangs were getting more and more difficult to manage, and there were times in the late 1970s and 1980s when the gangs even appeared to be control of the prisons. Gang leaders such as Larry Hoover not only became legends but also became so powerful within the prison walls that institutional wardens felt they had to stay on the good side of these inmates just to maintain peace within the joint. This environment encouraged wardens to begin negotiating with gang leaders, a topic that will receive more attention in a following chapter.

Doing Time

In his early years of doing time, several significant factors were at play in Rico's life. First, he had to survive in a correctional system that was filled with youthful members from a variety of Chicago gangs. In 1971, Rico was sent to Stateville Correctional Center, which had several thousand inmates. As Johnnie Walton Sr. put it,

"It was extremely hard core at that time. Either you were a fighter or you were a punk, and there was no in between!"

Walton described Rico in this period: "Little 'Rico' Johnson weighed about 140 pounds, soaking wet, but he walked around Stateville like he weighed 300 pounds." He indicated that Rico had learned to fight well in the "Youth Reformatory Schools," such as St. Charles and Sheridan, but added that in the adult prisons, such as Pontiac and Stateville, an inmate had to be good with a home-made knife, or shank, because conflict was no longer limited to hand-to-hand fighting. The inmate had to be light on his feet and always have the means to protect himself.

According to Walton, what made Rico different was that "he was extremely quick and could out-think the average penitentiary 'con.' What made Rico really unique was the fact that he had a way of communicating with friends and enemies alike!" Walton went on to note that Rico "had a way of drawing even our arch rivals close to him to offer a glimmer of peace or alliance, only to turn right around and crush those that might be a future threat!"[3]

In his correspondence with me, Johnnie Walton stated that he went to Stateville after Rico was imprisoned there and that Rico wanted him to live in C-House with him because he had heard about Walton's "rep" (reputation) while at the Pontiac correctional center from 1969 to 1972: Rico only wanted the best fighters with him. Walton reported he was honored that Rico wanted him, but Bobby Gore, their "supreme chief," said "that he wanted me over in E-House with him so he could watch 'my little young wild bad ass.'"[4]

So, Walton reported, he and Rico were unable to team up and go on a rampage at Stateville. But they *were* together on some days. He wrote:

> [Rico] knew he had power to move people even back then! We were walking by the baseball diamond in Stateville, and the bleachers held about two thousand guys! So I said, "Rico, I see all of the Blackstone Rangers," because

3. Letter from Walton, December 2001.
4. Ibid.

> I [could] see the Red Scarfs they were bearing even back then. There were about three or four hundred Blackstone Rangers in the bleachers piled together, watching the game. I said, "Now I see the Disciples," because there were three or four hundred of them with their blue scarfs on their heads. I said, "but where are the Vice Lords?" Little Rico said, "everybody you see without any scarfs on their heads are Vice Lords, because we don't have to wear anything on our heads to identify ourselves," and Little Rico hollered, "Behold," which was our war cry and to acknowledge each other, and the entire bleachers erupted! "Almighty, Vice Lords!"
>
> There was over a thousand or more guys standing and screaming "Almighty Vice Lords" and Little Rico Johnson smiled and said, "Now that's the Power of the Lords!"

In his correspondence, Walton then moved to the organizational structure of the Vice Lords at that time. He said the magazines *Ebony* and *Jet* reported that the gang had 40,000 members and twenty to twenty-three branches. Each branch had its president, vice president, and chief war counselor. "Our big three," according to Walton, were "Bobby Gore, our president, 'Jew Boy' (later called the Mandi), our vice president, and Little Rico (later called the Minister), our chief war counselor and our third in command."[5] Walton added: "Our brother Pep was our founder and first President, and his ingenious mind, leadership and charisma, is what started the entire thing off, and we have to take our hats off to this Brother, but Bobby Gore, Jew Boy, and Little Rico Johnson took our entire Nation of Lords to another level."[6]

A second change in the Vice Lords in the early 1970s was a new emphasis on education in the prisons. Ever since arriving at Stateville in 1971, Gore had wanted to start a process to educate the Vice Lord inmates and have each develop a skill before they were released. Rico got his GED and went on to get associate's and

5. Ibid.
6 Ibid.

bachelor's degrees as well. He went to barbering school first and then worked in the sheet-metal vocational shop.

A third change in this period was that drugs were introduced in the community and in the prison. The Vice Lords were divided into their branches by the late 1960s and 1970s, and interbranch relations deteriorated because of warring over the distribution of drugs. So, following the social outreach programs from 1967 to 1970, which had offered the hope that gangbangers could become community organizers and activists, it was now drug distribution and sales that motivated gang activities. This not only resulted in huge jumps in violence but also led to alienation among the various branches.

An example of this gang rivalry would be fully documented a few years later when Willie Lloyd, chief of the Unknown Vice Lords, aspired to be head of the Vice Lord Nation. The Conservative Vice Lords, of course, had little interest in giving up their role as head of the Nation. Soon, a hit was ordered on Lloyd, and several attempts were made on his life, one of which paralyzed him. In 2014, as earlier noted, he was slain while walking his dogs near his Minneapolis home.

A fourth change would occur in the mid-1970s when the Vice Lords became Muslims. Chapter 5 tells how this took place in Rico's life. As a boy, he had had little or no response to the Baptist church attended by his mother. However, his newfound faith had tremendous impact on his life. He found redemption when he became a Muslim and led his Vice Lord brothers to this faith.

5

Beliefs and Practices of Islam— The First Redemptive Script

Rico Johnson was attempting to establish his leadership role in the Vice Lords and, at the same time, to keep anyone from "messing" with him. Then in 1973 at the Pontiac Correctional Center, he met Joseph Ussef, beginning a relationship that would change his life. Ussef had converted to Islam sometime before. When he met Rico Johnson, he realized that this young brother needed to change his life and that in doing so he could influence other African American inmates to change theirs as well. Accordingly, Ussef began exposing Rico to the teachings and practices of Islam.

Johnson at best had been a nominal Baptist, but this Protestant religion had little or no appeal for him. Yet influenced by the charisma and commitment of Joseph Ussef, he soon became a convert to Islam. He had had some exposure to the faith during his first imprisonment at Pontiac, but it was his time with Joseph that made the difference. The two men were only together for a few months before Rico was transferred to Stateville, but throughout both of their long prison careers, Joseph faithfully continued his mentoring relationship, their letters going back and forth. In fact,

Joseph has maintained his relationship with Rico to the present day.

To understand the impact of a religious experience, it is helpful to examine the practices one pursues, the beliefs one has, and the commitment one extends to this religious reality in one's life.

Practices

Early on during his instruction from Ussef, Rico adopted a new dress code and stopped eating pork. He began praying five times a day. He also observed the *wudo* (purification) and religious holidays. Energized by his new beliefs, he wanted Islam to be accepted throughout the Vice Lord Nation. Bobby Gore was also brought into Islam, and by 1975, the process of establishing Islam had spread throughout the penitentiary system. Within five years, the VLN had accepted a new religious system.

Beliefs

Eventually, Rico prepared a pamphlet on Islam for use by all members of the Vice Lord Nation. In this pamphlet, he defined what it means to devote oneself to Islam, and he discussed the Islamic prayer, the five pillars of Islam, the principles of the articles of faith, the oath of the Almighty Lords of Islam, statements on love and the flag, and the obligations required of each member of the Nation of Islam. The statement of beliefs is the following:

EXCERPTS FROM

THE HOLY QURAN

OF THE

LORDS OF ISLAM

(**5**)

Lords Of Islam

They are shaped into concrete forms to suit the times and circumstances according to the various needs of the average man and woman. Whether there be a need for clean and wholesome food; abolishment of blood feuds; charity to the poor, weak, and needy; refraining from wrong doings; learning self denial by fasting; having courage to fight for right; or banishing rioting, drinking, and gambling for example. All of these are the goals and guidelines of 'The Almighty Lords Of Islam Nation'.

Waste not, nor misuse your life. Time through the ages bears witness that nothing remains but faith, good deeds, truth, patience, and perseverance. But for these, man against time is loss.

Take not your oaths to practice deception between yourselves, with the result that someone's foot may slip after it was firmly planted, ye may have to taste the evil consequences of having hindered men from the path of God, and a mighty wrath descend on you!

Islam is designed to appeal to our intellect so that we will be able to make the best use of our lives. Our religion is more than just a religion of faith, it is a rational religion of knowledge and logic. It is the fulfillment of the missions of all the prophets who led society to a faith that recognizes the existence of the 'One Creator' and the obligation of every creature to him.

Allah's grace and mercy are always first, but his justice and wrath will seize those who defy his *law*, and the *law* is Islam!

Al-Fatiha

The strong essence of the Islamic prayer and Islam itself is the first Sura (chapter) in the Holy Qur'an called Al-Fatiha (the opening). It is the key that unlocks understanding of the entire book. All meetings, spiritual or business, are opened and closed with this prayer. Learn it!

1. With the name Allah, most gracious, most merciful
2. All praise is due to Allah, the Lord of all the Worlds
3. Most gracious, most merciful, Master of the day of judgment
4. Thee do we worship and thine aid do we seek
5. Show us the straight way
6. The way of those upon whom thou hast bestowed thy grace
7. Those whose portion is not wrath and who go not astray

Five Pillars of Islam

Just as we have fundamental beliefs in Islam, we also have five fundamental practices which we must observe. By increasing our knowledge of these fundamentals we increase our understanding of Islam. These fundamental practices are the pillars upon which a Muslim's entire life is structured on, the Holy Qur'an and the Sunnah of Prophet Muhammad (PBUH).

The man of faith holds fast to his faith, because he knows it is true. The man of the world rejects faith, clings hard to worldly interest, and lets his mind think on worldly interests. But let him not force his interest on men, sincere and true, by favor, force, or fraud!

Let not man be intoxicated with power or material resources

. . .

Trust. Assured reliance on the character, ability, strength, or truth of someone or something

Loyalty. Faithful in allegiance to one's lawful government

Light. Something that makes vision possible

Concern. Marked interest or regard arising through a personal tie or relationship

Business. A recurring recession of fluctuations in activity

The Five Pillars of Islam

1. Shahada (testifying that there is no God but Allah and that Muhammad is his prophet)

2. Salat (prayer) at least five (5) times daily

3. Zakat (charity)

4. Saum (fasting) especially during the month of Ramadhan

5. Haji (pilgrimage) to Mecca at least once in one's lifetime

Articles of Faith (Islamic Principles)

The fundamental 'Principles of Islam' are the most important things in a Muslim's life. We should not look for ways to modify the 'Principles of Islam' to justify unlawful and unnatural practices. We are to alter our practices and attitudes to conform to Islamic Principles.

Articles of Faith

1. Belief in the oneness of Allah (God)

2. Belief in all of the Prophets

3. Belief in the Books of Allah

4. Belief in the Angels of Allah

5. Belief in the Day of Resurrection (life after death)

6. Belief in the Divine Ordinance (that all powers proceed from Allah, but that we're responsible for our own actions)

Almighty Lords Of Islam

We 'The Almighty Lords Of Islam Nation' will continue to represent our beloved Nation throughout these times when only those who are not pure in heart will be overcome by the common enemy whose proper name is 'ROME'. We the people of 'The Almighty Lords Of Islam Nation' will devote our time and greatest effort to advance all poor and oppressed people within our reach. We the people of 'The Almighty Lords Of Islam Nation' will greet and honor each representation with greetings of plain palms out and upward who identify with the cause that we will never cause any action or harm to one another nor shall we cause division among the people of 'The Almighty Lords Of Islam Nation' . . . give ALL PRAISE TO ALLAH, for he is the Father.

Continuation of Love, Truth, Peace, Freedom, and Justice!

We Remain Almighty Lords Of Islam

Mankind was one single nation and God sent messengers with glad tidings and warnings. With them he sent the 'Book Of Truth' to judge people on matters when they disagreed. But the people of the book, after the clear signs came to them, they did not differ among themselves, except through selfish contumacy. God by his grace guided the believers to the truth, concerning that wherein they differed, for God guides whom he will to a path that is straight.

Key Point

To each I a goal to which Allah turns him, then strive together as in a race towards all that is good where so ever ye are. Allah will bring you together, for Allah hath power over all things.

'The Almighty Lords Of Islam Nation' Oath

In the name of 'The Almighty' I so solemnly swear that I, as a Representative of 'The Almighty Lords Of Islam Nation' will not dishonor my most sacred weapon, meaning UNITY, nor under the threat of death will I deny those who stand beside me.

I as a Representative of 'The Almighty Lords Of Islam Nation' will listen well to the truthful teachings of our Elites. I will serve my time constructively while imprisoned, so that upon my release I will be a productive citizen for myself and my community.

Let the Almighty God (Allah) bear witness to this oath, by birth in spirit, and throughout the hearts' core, I come as I am, to 'The Almighty Lords Of Islam Nation.'

'Lord Love' means I have an undying love for 'The Almighty Lords Of Islam Nation' and I'll die for it.

All Praise!

All praise to the Elites, sons of the almighty and righteous warriors and prophets of *'Lords of Islam'*. All praise to the Elites, Lord of Lords . . . Lords of the world. All praise to the Elites who suffered through what the enemy had, and will now lead their people to victory against the same enemy. All praise to the Elites, the way, the truth, the light, and through them comes knowledge, wisdom, and understanding of *'Lords of Islam'*.

Behold Lords Of Islam!

Under the golden sun the double edged sword drips with the blood of our enemies, all praise to the Elites. We are 'Lords of Islam' and the double edge sword is in the hand of the children of Allah who are worthy of wearing the king's crown. We are the 'Lords of Islam' and the hands of Allah will guide and keep us on the path of righteousness, always fighting to become mentally free, as well as physically. We are the 'Lords of Islam' . . . Lords of the World; it is our duty to teach, protect, and represent all poor and oppressed people nation wide.

In the name of Allah, we swear never to dishonor our most sacred weapon (meaning Lord Unity), nor under the threat of death will we deny those who stand beside us. Come out of the darkness and let the golden rays glitter upon your armor of war, the double edge sword and the righteous warriors battle dress of 'Pure Gold'. All honor to the Elites, Lords of Lords and Prophets of 'Lords of Islam'. Lords of the World, Behold! ALMIGHTY LORDS OF ISLAM.

"Behold", the Lord said to the Angels, "I will create a vicegerent on the earth". They said, "Will thou place therein one who will make mischief therein and shed blood. Whilst we do celebrate thy praises and glorify thy holy name."

In the name of the Almighty Allah, we the people of 'The Almighty Lords Of Islam Nation' give praise to the Supreme Elites, Amani and our Elites, righteous sons of the 'The Almighty Lords Of Islam Nation'!

Behold! Hear our prayer O' Lords of Lords and give us your people, 'The Almighty Lords Of Islam Nation', the continued courage to represent our beloved Nation so that the world will know that we are the 'Lords of Islam' and as such will never stray from our 'Divine Principles and Concepts', the law by which we the most righteous of your people live.

By your divine grace and generosity you have instilled within us, thy divine seed of love, knowledge, wisdom, and understanding. As representatives of 'The Almighty Lords Of Islam Nation', it is our responsibility to apply these precious gifts to the best interest of our beloved Nation, and all poor and oppressed people of color nationwide. It is known if we retrogress from thy 'Divine Principles of Law', the wrath of this 'The Almighty Lords Of Islam Nation' will surely fall upon us; for we have pledged to give our Love, Life, and Loyalty to this 'The Almighty Lords Of Islam Nation'. Let our conduct of the '*Lords of Islam*' be judged accordingly.

For whom else among us is more worthy of wearing the king's crown than our Supreme Elite, Amani and the Elites, righteous sons of the Almighty, and the Prophets of '*Lords of Islam*'. Lords of the World, Lords of the World, Behold! Almighty '*Lords of Islam*'.

<u>Note:</u> What remains if you deny all faith and personal responsibility? Why then help the helpless or teach others deeds of charity, vain where worship without heart and soul? What you think of men who make great show, but fail to meet the simple needs of daily life?

Statement of Love

For you my Brother, my love began at your birth and has manifested throughout our heritage because of our 'Black Skin' which is just, your blood and flesh which is us. I am you and you are me! Our efforts for the same cause, our minds for the same goal, our lives for a new nation, our souls bound for the same destination. For this cause I give all my unity and vitality, for you I give All my Love!

The Flag

The following is a written breakdown of the Nation's Flag and what some of you call the 'Emblem'. The flag is a symbol of knowledge relating to parts of our Black History and cultural position.

The flag is the national identification for any nation of people. It is what the people represent and live for. This flag is the symbol of the entire 'Lords of Islam Nation' and consists of the following:

Circle. The circle means 360 degrees of knowledge and what was will always be. Black People once ruled the world and will once again, rule.

Fire. The circle is surrounded by fire. The fire represents our Nation's true knowledge of themselves is being suppressed. The flames prevent us from reaching 360 degrees of knowledge because of the heat (ROME)!

Darkness. Inside the circle is darkness or "jet black" and this represents that universally Black People are a majority people not a minority. Note: If we were not brainwashed into thinking we are different than other Blacks around the world, we would have a population of over SEVEN HUNDRED MILLION! There are four hundred million Blacks in the Africa, the motherland alone! Black also represents the darkness we have kept inside.

Moons. Inside the darkness are two crescent moons. They represent the splitting of one nation into two; one in the East (Asia, Egypt, Africa, etc.), the other in the West (us).

Star. Also, in this darkness is a golden star. This is the eye of Allah keeping watch over his people. A just/justice seeking people.

Pyramid Triangle. The darkness also engulfs the 'Pyramid Triangle', which is our strength. It is the phenomenon that puzzles the White world today. There is still no knowledge of pyramid building today, even with all the technology of the White Man's world. Society can't even begin to build or understand how to build the pyramid, yet the pyramid was built by Black People. We, 'The Almighty Lords Of Islam Nation' are sheltered by this pyramid of strength, until we are able to cleanse our mind. There are three aspects to the formation of the mighty puzzling pyramid. They are physical, mental, and spiritual knowledge. We must decide now how we want to live. Are we going to let our physical cravings take control of our minds? Or are we going to control our bodies as it is supposed to be? MIND OVER MATTER!

<u>Sun.</u> Inside the pyramid is the Sun. This represents the rising of truth in our nation once our minds have gained control over our physical bodies. We will then think as men and be able to understand and respect one another's life position. Then we can move as men (one) in a righteous direction. We, like all Black People are living within the shelter of the pyramid, under the watchful eye of Allah, are guided down the proper path.

<u>Hat.</u> The hat represents the sheltering of our heads until we can get them together. It also represents the fact that we are conservative in our thinking.

<u>Cane.</u> The cane is our 'Staff of Strength', (we need the cane to help us walk when we are old). The cane represents the need for 'us' to support one another in these trying times.

<u>Gloves.</u> The gloves represent purity which we will keep our hand clean of any act that causes division among our people. This is also the reason for representing as we do now (palms out and upward), which shows each other that our hands are clean: I MEAN YOU NO WRONG!

The Rules

1. The chain of command within this society will be maintained so the Elites will be able to devote their time and efforts to the major concerns and functions of the Nation. The administration will be qualified to handle all types of situations and problems that may surface or anything dealing with the Representatives of 'The Almighty Lords of Islam Nation'. The administration will also be qualified to deal with situations pertaining to other organization problems. That administration will be set by headquarters and will not be altered without his knowledge. The Watch Elite will be appointed to his proper field of work. All of these Elites will also be appointed by headquarters and will demonstrate and perform

their duties/jobs to the utmost and highest manner of 'The Almighty Lords of Islam Nation'. Failure of an Elite to perform in the highest manner will result in him being judged according to the *law*.

2. Each society will be placed with a location Elite, Minister of Command, Minister of Literature and Location Lieutenant, if necessary. These brothers will work hand-in-hand with one another to demonstrate the same exact *law* of 'The Almighty Lords of Islam Nation'. If any of the administration is charged and found guilty of demonstrating any other *law*, they will be judged accordingly.

3. The Administration will not tolerate different branches. Each location Elite will be viewed by headquarters and debriefed on the plans set for the movement of 'The Almighty Lords of Islam Nation'. The Elite over the entire society will be the most trustworthy, honored, respectable, dedicated, and sincere in making this Nation as a whole work. The *law* governs the society. He is there to make sure the *law* is being administered in a just manner.

4. One priority of each location Elite is to make time for the younger brothers in order to teach lessons in the signs of 'The Almighty Lords of Islam Nation'. These are the signs in which this Nation moves forth, anything else will not be constructive for the Representatives, therefore, it is not to be demonstrated. If one is charged with improper demonstrating and found guilty, he will be judged accordingly.

5. Every order given from a location Elite will never be questioned unless the individual receiving the order doesn't understand the order that is being given. No location Elite will ever put himself, or any Representative in a situation where he will be disrespected. Also neither he or any Representative will be disrespected by any other man, in or out of this organization.

6. As long as every Representative or location Elite is in accord with the *laws* of 'The Almighty Lords Of Islam Nation',

everyone will give his full and undivided attention to the brother, or the Elite because this is showing respect to the other individual and it shows 'Unity'. THE LAW GOVERNS ALL EVENTS.

7. The only location an Elite may speak on matters pertaining to the Nation is his own location. He can only give his constructive advice on any other location and this is something that has to be approved by that particular location Elite.

8. Each Elite and Representative of 'The Almighty Lords Of Islam Nation' will be notably respected because as 'Lords of Islam', we demand our respect by our actions and deeds. Representatives disrespecting each other will come to a halt.

9. Each location Elite, along with each Representative will keep notice of their appearance. They will always appear neat and clean. In 'The Almighty Lords Of Islam Nation' this *law* will be enforced daily.

10. The Minister of Literature within a particular location will be under the influence of the Minister of the entire society. The Minister of each location's responsibility is to assure all Representatives of 'The Almighty Lords Of Islam Nation's' *law*. He is literally to carry himself like a minister. He is to be available at all times to the Nation and Representatives to help them to understand the ISLAM religion. They will inform all the Representatives of the *law*—ISLAM, AND THE LAW WILL PREVAIL. Each minister will know all of the literature that is required and he will do his best in teaching the Representatives within his location.

Note: The Minister of Literature's only responsibility is to teach all Representatives the religion of Islam and our Nation's literature. Disrespecting a minister for any reason is a serious violation of 'The Almighty Lords Of Islam Nation' *law*!

11. If any Elite, Minister, or Representative is charged and found guilty of demonstrating in signs other than 'The Almighty Lords Of Islam Nation', they will be judged accordingly.

12. Every Friday when Juma'r services are being held, all Elites, Ministers, and Representatives will attend these services unless their job makes it impossible for them to attend—WE DO MEAN IMPOSSIBLE! Each location's Minister of Literature will assure each Representative of the proper dress code (no sweat suits, no braids in hair, no plastic bags on heads, and everyone will have on a blue shirt and clean socks). The Elite will be held responsible for brothers not attending.

13. During the week, all Elites and Ministers of Literature will find a place in their own location to hold studies on Islam, which is to be directed by the Minister of Literature. There will also be classes on the literature and truthful teachings of 'The Almighty Lords Of Islam Nation'. Elites and Representatives may take part if they have something constructive to offer.

14. If any Elite, Minister, or Representative <u>cannot</u> fulfill his obligation because he is under the influence of or has a drug problem, it will be upon the Elite and Minister of the society and the Elite of that particular location to take a vote to determine whether or not that Elite, Minister, or Representative is to be placed under arrest. (In this day and time we cannot afford to deal with the problem of trying to teach the younger brothers in our community when the spear head dwell in something that constantly alters the state of his mind.) If we allowed this behavior from our heads we risk destroying everything we have worked so hard for.

15. If brothers fail to meet the high standards of 'The Almighty Lords Of Islam Nation' and they continue to misuse, flaunt our '<u>Divine Principles/Concepts</u>' and make us ashamed; it will be upon the Elites of the Society to make the decision of arresting the particular individual upon hearing statements from the Elite of that particular location. We have no time for

individuals who threaten or stunt our growth no matter who the individual may be!

16. Every Elite, Minister, and Representative will have the right to speak or voice his opinion on programs or anything that will make 'The Almighty Lords Of Islam Nation' grow, whether it pertains to their location or if it is suitable for the entire society.

17. If at any time a Representative wants to remove himself from the Nation, it will be upon the Elite of the Society to grant this request from the Representatives. Note: We will not force anyone to be part of 'The Almighty Lords Of Islam Nation'.

18. The only Elites within any location who will be active and functioning are those who are stated by headquarters. Their concern is for the overall movement of this Nation, not their own prestige.

19. While attending Juma'r service, everyone will be seated inside where the service is being held. There will be no one out in the hallway during the service, except for the Representatives on security. No meetings will be held during Juma'r Service!

20. The slavery workers will look on the welfare of our Representatives in slaver (orientation). They will inform the Elite of the Society how many Representatives are in slavery and also make sure the Representatives get all of their property and everything they have coming!

21. All location problems will stay among its location. No Elite, Minister, or Representative is ever to take a problem from one location to another pertaining to 'The Almighty Lords Of Islam Nation' unless the problem in that particular location cannot be handled and assistance is required. Therefore if necessary, the Elite of the location shall report to the Elite of the Society.

22. At no time will any Elite have four (4) or five (5) brothers as his personal security; there is no such thing. 'The Almighty

Lords Of Islam Nation' has no room for anyone who is afraid of a mere man!

23. No Elite, Minister, or Representative shall ever overlook our main purpose which is to be an organization throughout these times. Our objective is to be sincere about what we believe in and what we will die for. We aim to show the world what we stand on!

24. Representatives will follow the guidelines that have been established throughout our 'Laws and Principles'. Nothing less will be accepted from any Elite, Minister, or Representative of 'The Almighty Lords Of Islam Nation'.

25. Any Elite, Minister, or Representative that has six months or longer and does not have a "High School Diploma", will enroll in the GED program. All brothers that are not enrolled in college courses or vocational program will be expected to have a job, within or anywhere outside of their living unit.

26. Every member of 'The Almighty Lords Of Islam Nation' will obey the 'Code of Conduct'. In the past brothers have failed to honor parts of the 'Code of Conduct' as if it never existed. This will be maintained at all times throughout the entire society.

27. Each Representative, upon reaching a particular location will be given the policy of that location by the location Elite. The Representative will also be given the *laws* of 'The Almighty Lords Of Islam Nation' from the Minister of that location. He will be expected to learn them immediately.

28. A Representative will not take it upon himself to deal with a problem when it arises. He shall always contact the proper authority within his location to handle the problem. Taking things into your own hands (a representative) could lead to a bigger and/or possibly an even more dangerous problem.

29. Each Representative will be screened on his daily 'Laws and Principles' of 'The Almighty Lords Of Islam Nation'. He will

also be looked upon to carry himself in the signs or 'The Almighty Lords Of Islam Nation', in the highest form!

30. Any Representative that has potential and constructive ideas will be considered, no matter how young a brother might be.

31. Every Representative of 'The Almighty Lords Of Islam Nation' shall at all times maintain himself within the 'Code of Conduct', 'Chain of Command' and 'The Principles Of Law'.

32. Every 15th and 30th of the month, all location Elites will meet together to discuss plans, ideas, and goals upon their location and the society of 'The Almighty Lords Of Islam Nation'.

33. It shall be every Representative's sworn duty to uphold 'The Almighty Lords Of Islam Nation' in their location or wherever they may be where other Representatives are residents.

34. Upon entering meeting places, all drugs and alcoholic beverages will be left outside of the particular fort, because we need no reason to promote anything but the higher self and to be in the right frame of mind!

35. Every Representative of 'The Almighty Lords Of Islam Nation' will be in tune with the precise chain of command, CHIEF ELITE, MINISTER OF JUSTICE AND ELITES. This is the only chain of command that will be honored by every Representative of 'The Almighty Lords Of Islam Nation'.

36. It is every location Elites' sworn duty to direct all Representatives in a positive/productive direction of 'The Almighty Lords Of Islam Nation'.

37. Every Representative after being given the 'Laws and Principles' of 'The Almighty Lords Of Islam Nation' will never stray from the principles which we stand by and DIE for!

38. Every Elite will have open communication with all locations in case his assistance is needed in an emergency.

39. The Chief Elite will maintain an accurate account of all location Elites. He and the Minister of Justice will be the only

authority to call upon any other location and their Representatives if needed.

40. We, the Representatives of 'The Almighty Lords Of Islam Nation' should stop worrying about the threat we seem to think we pose to each other's personal prestige and concentrate on our unified efforts towards solving the unending hurt that is being done daily to our community, family, and representatives.

41. We, 'The Almighty Lords Of Islam Nation' will put our accent upon the youth; we need new ideas, new methods and approaches. We shall call upon the young Representatives of the truthful teachings that are following the clear footsteps to help us.

42. As Representatives of 'The Almighty Lords Of Islam Nation' we must seek to find solutions for the betterment of all our people. We must solve and duly prepare our people for the struggle ahead because there can be no progress without a struggle!

43. As Representatives of 'The Almighty Lords Of Islam Nation', we must learn to love the people who paved the way for us to walk the path of righteousness. We must learn to love and respect other representatives' life principles if they differ from our own.

44. All Representatives of 'The Almighty Lords Of Islam Nation' must understand, instead of arrogance there will be humility among other representatives. Instead of power drunkenness, there will be strong realization to serve 'The Almighty Lords Of Islam Nation'!

45. Representatives of 'The Almighty Lords Of Islam Nation' will be guided by the tenets (doctrine) of morality and the 'Divine Principles of Love' that show the world, we are Lords of the World.

46. All Representatives of 'The Almighty Lords Of Islam Nation' will be powerful and effective, no one will be more. No one

can or will be more powerful than HE WHO FEARS NONE BUT GOD and seeks blessings from none but him!

47. All Representatives of 'The Almighty Lords Of Islam Nation' will do justice to all sundry (various, miscellaneous), discharge his duties honestly and work for the good of the Nation.

48. All Representatives of 'The Almighty Lords Of Islam Nation' will be fair, straight, forward and honest in his dealings.

49. No Representatives will ever be a party to oppression or violation of anyone's life and will honor whatever their form or color.

50. All Representatives of 'The Almighty Lords Of Islam Nation' will uphold Truth even at the cost of his Life!

Principles Of Law

I, as a Representative of 'The Almighty Lords Of Islam Nation', swear with my life never to dishonor our most High Chief, Minister of Justice, Elites, or any other Representative of 'The Almighty Lords Of Islam Nation'.

I, as a Representative of 'The Almighty Lords Of Islam Nation', which teach our people, protect our people, love our people, and if it is the will of our Almighty God, Allah, die for our people so that one day they will walk the golden path of '_Lords of Islam_' as free people, as productive people, as people progressing in the love of '_Lords of Islam_', the knowledge of '_Lords of Islam_', this wisdom of '_Lords of Islam_', the understanding of '_Lords of Islam_, the living '_Lords of Islam_'.

I, as a Representative of 'The Almighty Lords Of Islam Nation', will never stray from the truthful teachings of our most wise and beloved Elites.

I, as a Representative of 'The Almighty Lords Of Islam Nation', will help my people with any problem they may encounter, be it mentally or physically, for their problems are my problems, and my problems are theirs.

I, as a Representative of 'The Almighty Lords Of Islam Nation' will never take the words of another before the word of any Representative of 'The Almighty Lords Of Islam Nation'. This I swear upon the *'Lords of Islam'*.

I, as a Representative of 'The Almighty Lords Of Islam Nation', swear with my life I will never put anything or anyone before my Chief Elite, Minister of Justice, Elites, or any Representative of 'The Almighty Lords Of Islam Nation'; be it my life, my family, or associates.

I, as a Representative of 'The Almighty Lords Of Islam Nation', will never deny any *'Lords of Islam'* materially or spiritually under any circumstances or be denied.

I, as a Representative of 'The Almighty Lords Of Islam Nation', swear with my life that I will not lie on any Representative, fight any Representative, steal from any Representative, or take by force anything from any Representative of 'The Almighty Lords Of Islam Nation'.

Behold Almighty Lords of Islam

Code of Conduct

Respect. Every Elite, Minister, and Representative of 'The Almighty Lords Of Islam Nation' will at all times respect one another. Respect is to be extended to every representative in another organization. Every *'Lord of Islam'* will demand respect by his conduct, character, personal demeanor, actions, and deeds. Every Elite, Minister, and Representative of 'The Almighty Lords Of Islam Nation' is to respect all persons who are not representatives of any nation. Disrespect is a very serious violation of the 'Principles of Law' in our organization and it will not be tolerated, therefore, you will be judged accordingly.

Discipline. Discipline must and will be maintained for the successful functioning of the Nation. Every order you are given is to be carried out promptly and efficiently. Every order you are given is to be carried out promptly and efficiently. Every order received has a purpose and is not to be questioned unless a Representative does not understand the order being given (this is the only justification for questioning an order). Failure to carry out an order promptly and efficiently could endanger the life of yourself or other 'Lords of Islam'. For this reason, orders will be obeyed accurately! Failure to do so will result in immediate disciplinary action appropriate for the situation.

Meetings. General meetings of 'The Almighty Lords Of Islam Nation' are held for the purpose of the Nation business. The meetings will be conducted with the Elite first to state the business of the Nation. Secondly, followed by the members of the administration of the Nation. And finally, each Representative will be given the opportunity to speak about germane matters (relevant to the point at hand) in the meeting.

When any 'Lord of Islam' is speaking during a meeting, all others will remain quiet and attentive. Failure to do so constitutes disrespect, which will result in immediate disciplinary action. All problems pertaining to any location shall first be discussed when important factors are being discussed.

All Elites, Ministers, and Representatives will remain on his square and are to refrain from smoking while the meeting is in progress at all times. All Elites and Ministers will attend location meetings unless their occupation makes it impossible.

Dues. 'The Almighty Lords Of Islam Nation' boxes are established for the benefit of every 'Lord of Islam'. These boxes help during times of hardship we may experience. They are there to help our families and ourselves at those times. Therefore, dues will be paid by every 'Lord of Islam' monthly. 'The Almighty Lords Of Islam Nation' dues will be paid on the 15th of each month unless an exception has been made by the location Elite. Failure of any Elite, Minister, or Representative to pay dues will result in a loss of box privilege, and possible disciplinary action.

If it is impossible for a Representative to pay his monthly dues, he will complete constructive service for the Nation. Anything taken from the box for personal use must be replaced no later than the 15th of the following month. If a Representative has paid dues (keep an accurate record), he has the right to borrow funds to be used for constructive use. These boxes are for the use and benefit of every 'Lord of Islam'!

Horseplay. Horseplay is one of the principle causes leading to disrespect which can result in other serious problems. Therefore to avoid such problems, horseplay will be kept to a minimum. The yard and gym is the place for recreation. The manner in which a 'Lord of Islam' conducts himself reflects not only on him, but the entire organization of 'The Almighty Lords Of Islam Nation'.

Fighting. No member of 'The Almighty Lords Of Islam Nation' should place himself in a situation that will involve fighting over trivial matters. If an attack occurs on any Representative, it is the sworn duty/obligation of every 'Lord of Islam' to overcome the attackers by any means necessary.

If any of the Elites, Ministers, or Representatives are fighting among themselves, it is a violation of the *laws* of 'The Almighty Lords Of Islam Nation' and it will be dealt with immediately. Fighting is only authorized between Representatives in the circle with boxing gloves as allowed by 'The Almighty Lords Of Islam Nation'.

Movement. If at anytime you have a change of housing, cell, location, or work transfer, you are to notify the location Elite of the transfer as soon as possible. To maintain security and ensure ready access to all 'Lords of Islam', it is mandatory we are always aware of the work and assignment location of each member. After moving anywhere in the institution, each specific location will move as one in a uniform way.

Summary. This 'Code of Conduct' was established to maintain security, discipline, safety, and the integrity of 'The Almighty Lords Of Islam Nation'. You are expected to know and obey this code at all times. Caution: Be aware of your surroundings and the people around you at all times! Remember who and what you are, so conduct yourself accordingly.

Chain Of Command

The following is the Administrative Organization of 'The Almighty Lords Of Islam Nation'. This 'Chain Of Command' shall be followed at all times.

Chief Elite. He has authority over the entire body of 'The Almighty Lords Of Islam Nation'. He is the chief decision maker. The main objective of the Chief Elite is to formulate the 'Laws and Rules' of this organization and to keep it moving in a positive and constructive manner no matter what the circumstances or environment may be.

Minister of Justice. He determines right (justice) from wrong (injustice) on a balanced scale. He will speak on the behalf of the Chief Elite. He will make sure all members of 'The Almighty Lords Of Islam Nation' are treated right at all times. He is the only one authority to take orders from the Chief Elite and is to make sure they are carried out efficiently and accurately. He and the Elites are the only ones authorized to approach the Chief Elite with problems pertaining to 'The Almighty Lords Of Islam Nation'.

Elites. Each Elite will be assigned to a particular location which he will have complete authority over. For example, if an Elite is in charge of 'The Almighty Lords Of Islam Nation's' finance; his responsibilities are to oversee with the finance department, to carry himself in the highest manner as a *'Lord of Islam'* and to give positive and constructive advice when asked by another Elite. He is to be always respected and honored. If an emergency arises and the Chief Elite nor the Minister of Justice can be reached, then the nearest Elite is to make an immediate decision.

Minister of Command. These chosen men are the Elites. However, there are certain situations where a Representative can and will fill this position, if he is qualified and voted into the position by the location Elite. He is commanded to make sure the 'Laws and Rules' are functioning properly as ordered by the Chief Elite. The Minister of Command also has the authority to make a decision but not to the highest degree. He shall leave the most important decisions to the Chief Elite and the Minister of Justice.

Lieutenant. He is the assistant to the Minister of Command.

Minister. It is the Minister's dedicated duty to speak on the righteous and truthful aspects of the organization and the truthful teachings of our leaders. He is the spiritual leader of the movement and is to be respected as well as give respect to all the 'Lords of Islam'. He will only teach 'The Almighty Lords Of Islam Nation's' 'Laws and Principles' and should never demonstrate anything else!

Summary and Explanation. When the Chief Elite gives an order, he should discuss it with the Minister of Justice, which gives him his respect as the Chief Minister, the one who will neutralize/balance any problem that has occurred in 'The Almighty Lords Of Islam Nation' with the scale of right or wrong.

When a decision is made all the Ministers of Command will be called together and issues previously discussed by the Chief Elite and the Minister of Justice will be explained in detail. During this meeting each Minister of Command will be given an opportunity to speak on the issue. If all Ministers of Command are in agreement, then the decision will be told to the Lieutenants who will take it to every Representative they are in charge of in 'The Almighty Lords Of Islam Nation'.

Purpose Of Prayer

Prayer is the soul of all religions, and it has always formed an essential part of Islam. It is the symbol of humble reverence before the creator of the heavens, the earth, and everything above and below. Where there is no prayer there can be no purification of the soul. It is the remedy for the ills which beset the heart and corrupt the mind and soul.

Prayer in Al-Islam is a beautiful exercise in meditation through which we are able to forge a direct link with Allah. That it is not only an obligation but a gift and a privilege. When we neglect the worship of Allah we lose contact with Him and our sense of direction becomes faulty. We lose the spiritual guidance that comes from submission and obedience to Allah, and we become easy prey for evil influences which confront us throughout our daily lives. The spiritual vacuum created within us when prayer is neglected is soon filled with materialistic greed, prejudice, envy, jealousy, and other sins. A person who is affected loses his sense of humility before Allah and views himself as the ultimate authority in his life. He loses his sense of compassion for others and regards the wonders of Allah's creation only as they contribute to the fulfillment of his own selfish desires.

Prayer

What is the second 'Principle Of Islam'? The second 'Principles Of Islam' is to offer the Obligatory Prayers five (5) times a day.

What do you understand about prayer? Prayer is the act of worshipping Allah according to the teaching of the Holy Prophet.

What are the essential requisites for offering prayer? The essential requisites for offering prayer are:

1. The worshipper must be a Muslim.

2. The worshipper's clothes and body must be free from all impurities.

3. The place where the prayer is to be offered should be pure and clean. The part of the body between the navel and the knees of a male worshipper must be fully covered and the whole body except the hands and face of a female worshipper.

4. The worshipper must face the Ka'Ba in the Great Mosque at Mecca and the direction of Ka'Ba outside Mecca.

5. The worshipper must form the Niyyat (for example: intention) in his or her mind of the particular prayer, Fard (Obligatory) Sunnat or Nafi (Optional), he or she is about to offer.

6. The worshipper must observe the times and rules prescribed respective prayers.

7. The worshipper must have performed the Wudu (for example: ablution).

8. The worshipper must have performed Ghusi (for example: the washing of the whole body), if he or she was in a state of grave impurity.

Wudu (Ablution)

What is Wudu? Wudu is the act of washing those parts of the body which are generally exposed.

Aisha's Lessons

Minister Rico, who was known as Rahim by this point, also prepared a number of lessons for members of the Muslim Sisterhood. He wanted the sisterhood to read these lessons and meditate on them. The parables and concepts contained in Aisha's Lessons would guide them, Rahim asserted, into "individual, spiritual, and organizational development and growth." Their reward would be prosperity, and their pursuit of the right path would grant them "Peace, Justice, Mercy, Love, and Truth."

The Journey

Enlightenment, Rahim wrote, is one of the primary goals of the Aisha Sisterhood. "As you struggle to become free of the delusions of Satan," he advised, "you will rejoice in your human qualities, becoming more energetic, joyful and festive. Once established, there must be no alteration of course for you. Those who seek to appease and make friendship with sworn deceivers shall be sternly punished by their own foolishness."

Even more clearly, Rahim defined the purpose of the Sisterhood: "In the natural order of the universe, law governs all things. In law there is progress and there is deterioration. The Aisha Sisterhood means progress. The journey is now out of the wilderness and into light, prosperity, security and love. The quest of the journey is to become free of the delusions and to create the civilization within and without."

Division

Rahim warned that the Sisters will be destroyed if they lack knowledge and wisdom. He stated that many have been and continue to be enslaved because their visions "are not in agreement with the purpose for which we were created: to acknowledge truth, to seek justice and preserve the divine way." Those who fail to respond, whom Rahim called "mockers" and "scorners," will receive their compensation for their evil deeds. But for those who are faithful, Rahim affirmed that "Allah has promised the dew of heaven to refresh you, and he will again kiss the foreheads of those who refuse to kiss the hand of evil and idolatry."

The Conduct

Rahim went on to describe the conduct deemed appropriate for the Sisterhood: "The Aisha Sisterhood understands that the shedding of mental chains can only be accomplished by being open to the freedom from self-deception, being industrious, independent and honest with oneself and others while having a sincere desire to live in peace and prosperity, according to the Will of the Father. Having had a spiritual awakening, the Aisha Sisterhood is consistently seeking knowledge and wisdom, while conveying to others this awareness and by using their knowledge and skills to manifest enterprise, programs and small businesses throughout the community."

The House

In the closing section, Rahim warned that a house stands on the strength of its foundation. However, Satan is there to destroy the house; the House of God and the House of Satan are not made from the same mortar, nor can they be repaired with the same mortar. "The mortar of God," Rahim wrote, "is Truth and all its attributes and is obedient to the Will of the Spirit of Truth." By contrast, "the mortar of Satan is lust and wrath, hate and deceit, malice and every thing that harms, rather than those things and values that are obedient to truth and justice." A house built with the mortar of Satan "is designed to bring poverty, destruction and grief to the people of God." And he concluded that this House of Satan "will be destroyed by its own design."

Application to the Prison and Community

In 1975, after adopting Al-Islam, the Vice Lords developed therapy classes to explain how the faith would affect the community. As Rico put it, "We know that Islam was accepted because of the calmness and its positive nature that it brought to young men inside the prison system. As we continued to study it, we moved to a greater understanding of its beliefs and how it could be adopted in the prison and in the community."

When I asked Rahim how people on the outside accepted Islam, he replied, "It was rough at first. It was hard at first, but we kept persisting. We kept persisting, and then we found a way to make it work from the inside out to the community." He saw his role as teaching the brothers how to take Islam back to the community and educate the community about the faith. The first imam permitted to go into Stateville and teach from outside was Abdullah Muhammed.

Rahim added that his job was to enforce the law, which was Al-Islam, and make it work. He stated: "We would give classes on Islam. You would have three days of study period to learn Al-Fatiha [the first chapter of the Quran]. After three days, you would be faced with a disciplinary report if you did not know what you were supposed to. In seven days, you were expected to know Al-Fatiha and the five pillars."

Rahim said that converts were expected to become involved in educational and vocational programs. They were also expected to quit eating pork and the many things that had pork products in them. They had to adopt a new dress code and assume a new posture. For example, instead of a man putting his hands in front of his privates, he was supposed to stand at a 45-degree angle, holding his right hand over his left to keep his lower self in check. Rahim felt that these new disciplines brought something out of him that made him more productive and more spiritual than he had ever been in his life. "It made me not only want to be a productive citizen but to give back to some of those young men that I had taken from before. It made me want to help a lot of individuals."

Commitment

There are, of course, various levels of religious commitment, which partially explains why those who claim to be reborn sometimes lapse into questionable behavior. In the next chapter, we will see that after Rahim—to use the name he would adopt as a devotee of Allah—was paroled, he embarked on quite a rampage in the community. He violated his religious principles time after time as he robbed, intimidated, and even physically hurt individuals he encountered outside the prison walls.

How can this behavior be explained? Was it simply a shallowness in his commitment to Islam or an immaturity of faith? What happened to Rahim, who quickly reverted to being Rico the gangster in those months after he was released? He had been locked up for ten years, and the temptations of the street—the opportunities for crime, for profit, and for power in the gang—simply proved too much for him to resist.

Perhaps, as envisioned in Rico's religious system, Satan got hold of him and he succumbed. Yet when he was returned to prison in 1983 after his parole was revoked, he ardently repented. He was genuinely sorry for what he had done. This time, he was locked up for over thirty years, and appearance after appearance before the parole board only returned him to the cell block instead of the community. Despite this bleak outlook, the veracity of redemption in his later years of confinement was evidenced by the fact that he continued to reach out to others and serve as a positive influence in their lives.

Significantly, since he was at last released to the community in 2012, he has stayed faithful to his beliefs and to Allah. Today, he remains determined to do good for others, especially for the children of the community. His wonderful redemptive script remains intact, as will be documented in the chapters ahead.

6

Falling Off the Wagon

When Minister Rico was granted a parole from Logan Correctional Institution in Logan, Illinois, in October 1980, he felt that his attitude had changed and that he was ready to go home. On his release, Rico was really excited. His mother was still living, and he was looking forward to seeing her. Given $50 and a bus ticket by prison authorities, he traveled to Chicago alone: the authorities had taken him to the bus stop and left. Interestingly, as previously mentioned, when Willie Lloyd, chief of the Unknown Vice Lords, was released about this same time, he was greeted with a mink coat and a fleet of five stretch limos, courtesy of his gang.

Rico later recalled that when he got to his mother's home, "we just hugged and laughed and cried, and had fun." He spent the majority of the day with his mother, for he knew how much she had missed him. He saw his sisters and brother later that and following days.

The next thing Rico did after reconnecting with his family was to get a passport to go to Canada. It was the first time he had ever gotten a passport, and, as he remembered, it cost something like $13 or $26. At some point previously, Rico had gotten married, and he and his wife were going to visit his mother-in-law in Canada. She had a throat issue that caused her to be hospitalized, so they went to the hospital and stayed for two days to visit with her. Rico had been given a parole pass because he was still on parole at that time. He liked Canada and thought it was somewhere he would continue to visit.

But when Rico returned to Chicago, he was struck by all the turmoil and chaos he found there, stemming from the rampant drug trafficking. As he put it in one of our interviews, "I saw the nation going down. I had to do something, and the gangster came out. [I] felt that Islam had to be set aside in order to get on top of the situation." He went on:

> I realized that the drugs had become impregnated in the community. The young men of the community had become so wedded to the drugs that positive leadership would not make a difference. They were able to buy leadership, and they were buying and selling leadership of an organization like a piece of steak on a plate.... The separation of branches became a product of the influence of the drug money. The branches were getting established, stronger by the minute. So, by the time we woke up and found out what was happening, it was way too strong to stop it.

Rico felt that it was his job to bring the Vice Lord Nation up—and he needed to use whatever means that required. As his anger and frustration mounted over the next two years (from 1980 to early 1983), he ended up being involved in nine cases, seven murder charges, and one armed robbery. He concluded that he was past redemption at that point.

In discussing how out of control and antisocial he had become, he had this to say: "I had discipline, but I did not use discipline. I had socialization, but I did not use socialization. I became antisocial, and I think [for] the majority of my prison life I may [have been] more fearful of socialization than anything."

Asked why he was fearful of socialization, he responded, "When you study people for a long time, you have a tendency to look into the heart of people more so than the surface of them." In talking with people, he did not hear what they were saying, but he saw what they were doing. As Rico put it, "If your heart is speaking far away from your mouth, there are two different people talking to me. And I pay attention to the doer, not the talker."

Rico acknowledged that he may not be an Einstein, but he can read your life and know you. He is stressing his intuitive ability to understand people and see below the surface of things. He added that his ability to read people enabled him to develop their skills and potentials. Later on, this trait contributed to the ways in which he impacted a number of inmates before they went home. Interestingly, some of them have stayed away from crime for three decades or more.

However, in the two-plus years while he was paroled, what Rico expressed was his antisocial behavior. He was simply out of control, committing one crime after another. Johnnie Walton Sr. reported on what took place during those years:

> So Minister Rico was paroled and all hell broke loose. First of all, Minister Rico met the Gangster (Mafia) Boy's wife Paula, and married her, and after making parole, Minister Rico and his wife lived out in Downer's Grove, an affluent suburb of Chicago for a while. Most of us who knew Minister Rico knew that wasn't going to last, because Rico was brought up in the mean streets of Chicago, on the "ruffest and tuffest" street in Chicago, 16th Street!

In a letter to me, Johnnie Walton explained what was taking place with Rico:

> Minister Rico, like most of us who have served a long time in prison before release, have a whole lot of "wild oats" to sow, and we aren't going to sit still for very long. So, Minister Rico has finally made it back to the streets, but he has been gone for a long time, so he really doesn't know the full potential of the power that he has in his hands. . . . When the big three power structure was formed, Minister Rico was the "Minister of Justice," while Bobby Gore was known as the "Supreme Elite," and "Jew Boy" (Mandi) was known as the "Chief Elite." The Big Three was supposed to be like the President, the

Legislative Body, and the Supreme Court, with some kind of checks and balances along those lines, and while Minister Rico was the High Sheriff, or the man who carried out the law, he never had the opportunity to realize his leadership capacity or abilities back in his younger days!

Walton also provided a vivid description what happened when Rico returned to the community:

> So, when he touched down in the world, or "hit the streets," as we called it, it was harder for him to call the whole body of Vice Lords together in any meaningful, fully organized body, not as big and widespread as it was in 1980s, or even as it is today! With so many things going on, and some of the branch leaders being extremely powerful, with the narcotics game being in full swing, one had to be very careful on how he moved, or even what he said out of his mouth! . . . Now, by Minister Rico not being a fool, he put together a handful of the most treacherous group of thugs in the city, with his "right-hand man" being a guy everyone knew as "Hog Head." (I guess because he had an extremely large head.) Hog Head and some of the others, who had been out there in the streets for years, while Minister Rico was locked up, had convinced him that "the money was out there in the streets," which it was, and flowing like water, and it was all theirs for the taking! . . . Now, Minister Rico and his crew of thugs and roughnecks only numbered about thirty or so men, but it seemed like it was three hundred of them. They moved quickly and they moved viciously! They started robbing everything and everybody in sight! This was a wild-west show in its purest form! They did home invasions and pulled stunts that frighten the average hoodlum even to this day! They had the biggest guns, and they weren't afraid to use them. They robbed the toughest of the criminals out there on the streets, and anyone and everyone was a target or a threat to them!

The narration Walton offered in his letter continued:

It wasn't hard to keep up with the exploits of Minister Rico and his crew, because words traveled fast, and many of us wanted to keep up with the Minister and with what he was doing. So Minister Rico and Hog Head was the talk of the town, and all over the joints! Then, a few short months after his release, Minister Rico was arrested again, for a home invasion and armed robbery, and was convicted and sentenced to eighteen years in the Department of Corrections and was back with the real Vice Lord crew and in what we call "our second home."

Finally, Walton concluded by observing:

Getting locked up and convicted and sentenced this time might have saved Minister Rico's life, because shortly after he was convicted and sentenced, they found his right-hand man, Hog Head, savagely murdered and stuffed in a garbage can, as a message to what was left of Minister Rico's crew. The dope game was on and got bigger and more extreme, and some of the most cowardly guys in the streets started having tons of money, because either they had the organizational skills that Minister Rico and his crew lacked or they got lucky and found some of the best connections in the country!

In reading these excerpts from one of Walton's letters, three comments come to mind. First, I would consider whether his account is accurate or if it is an exaggerated retelling of events in the past. That Walton's account is authentic is suggested by the very fact that Johnnie showed Rico all the letters he was writing to me, coupled with the fact that Rico told me when I started his biography that the letters were an accurate rendering of what had taken place. Rico also validated this history in my interviews with him.

So, to use a word that Johnnie likes, Rico's few months on parole were a disaster. He got caught up in the drug business. He wanted to make hay while he could from the drug trade, and he also wanted to rob everyone in sight. Rico's months in the community validated what prison officials had been saying about him all along—he was lowlife and a thug at heart.

At some point during the years I was visiting Rico in prison and appearing before the parole board on his behalf, a friend of mine who had been the warden of facilities in which Rico was confined confronted me over the phone: "You have always been right on when it comes to understanding inmates. That is one of the things I like about you. Why have you been taken in by Johnson?" If I had talked with my friend following Rico's criminal rampage in the community, he no doubt would have said, "I told you so. We knew he was doing things in the prison when I was warden, but we just could not catch him."[1]

That I have written this biography and am accepting no royalties from it testifies to my belief in Rico Johnson and what he has accomplished and continues to accomplish with his life. However, I am fully cognizant of the huge impediments that come with growing up on the streets, becoming involved with gangs and crime, and gaining acceptance as a gang leader. So I am not surprised by what took place after Rico was paroled.

My second comment in response to Walton's correspondence is that his assertion about Rico being fortunate to have been returned to prison when he was rather than ending up in the cemetery is probably accurate as well. Gang leaders who have been incarcerated for a while and are paroled do not find a welcome on all fronts when they return to the streets. There is usually bloodshed, and the formerly respected gang chief may well find that the blood being shed is his own.

My third comment is that in Rico's mind, his conversion to Islam was a major turning point in his life, and he was influential in persuading at least the Conservative Vice Lords to become Muslims within a few years. What, then, happened to this redemptive script when he was paroled? Rico was a gangster—and a nasty one at that. There was certainly no evidence that his conversion to Islam had changed his life for the better.

Simply put, Rico fell off the wagon. But he was not the first person who professed great faith and then faltered or whose behavior contradicted the fervent religious declarations he or she

---

1. Phone conversation in January 1991.

had made. Therefore, it is critical to examine what took place *after* Rico fell off the wagon—or, to put it another way, to examine the sum total of his life.

When Minister Rico returned to prison in 1983, he found that things had changed there. The state had gained control of the prison, part of which meant they were able to control the gangs. What this meant is that Rico's power was much reduced from what it was before. Chapter 7 examines these changes.

7

Going Back to Prison

The prison system Rico returned to in 1983 was far different from the one that existed a decade earlier when he was first incarcerated. One major difference was that prison administrators had regained control of the prison in Illinois.

The Out-of-Control Prison

In a prison setting, control and order are similar but not the same thing. *Order* refers to a dynamic social equilibrium, which can be defined in the present context as "the absence of violence, overt conflict, or the threat of the chaotic breakdown of social routines." *Control* means a set of strategies or techniques used by prison administrators to achieve order.

In the orderly days of the past, convicts were told on the first day of confinement, both by staff and by other inmates, that they could do "easy time" or "hard time." The staff assured prisoners that troublemakers would lose whatever "good time" they had accumulated over the years. Good time is the amount of time deducted from a sentence after an inmate's admission to prison, contingent upon his or her behavior and attendance at classes and substance abuse treatment. The unwritten but powerful inmate code was useful both to prison administrators and to the prisoners themselves. The code promised order by encouraging inmates to serve their sentences without causing problems. Prisoners knew that disorder within the walls would mean the end of informal arrangements between inmate leaders and staff and the loss of privileges that may have taken them years to obtain.

Especially in the South, inmate trustees, sometimes called building tenders, were widely used to control other prisoners and perform many of the tasks ordinarily handled by custodial staff. Arizona, Mississippi, and Louisiana even permitted such inmates to carry firearms. Before the 1987 *Ruiz v. Estelle* decision rendered the building tenders system of the Texas Department of Corrections unconstitutional, inmate trustees in that state had been given authority by prison administrators to discipline other inmates who disturbed the social order.[1] The 1967 movie *Cool Hand Luke* realistically portrays what the situation was like for inmates in the South. Conditions were not much better in the prisons of the North, and in privatized facilities across the country, things were often much worse than in state-run facilities.[2]

Today, order has given way to disorder in many of the nation's prisons. A thriving contraband market, frequent and serious violations of rules and procedures, and more inmates choosing protective custody are all signs of the erosion of order. Fights, disturbances, and assaults are ever present, as are abuses, indignities, and more significant manifestations of disorder.

Various factors, including inmate gangs in forty states and the Federal Bureau of Prisons, the appetite for drugs among large numbers of prisoners, inmates serving longer sentences, and above all overcrowded conditions, combine to make it exceedingly difficult to restore order within these facilities. Since the 1980s, correctional officers have been quick to tell outsiders that the inmates are

1 *Ruiz v. Estelle*, 503 F. Supp. 1265 (S.D. Tex. 1980).

2. See Binder, *Bodies in Beds.*

running the institutions today, and in many prisons, this is more true than ever before.[3]

Although there have been many prison riots throughout history, the violence was to explode in nearly every large facility across the country after the 1971 Attica riot in upstate New York. The Attica riot began on Friday, September 9; by that evening, inmate leaders, realizing that their immediate demands were unrealistic, offered thirty-three proposals to authorities. In his meetings and communications with inmates over the weekend, Russell Oswald, the commissioner of correctional services, said he was committed to bringing the uprising to a peaceful resolution. He indicated that he could accept twenty-eight of the inmates' proposals and would do everything in his power to implement them. But he insisted on one condition of his own—the inmates had to release the hostages they were holding. On Monday morning, Oswald sent the inmates an ultimatum: release the hostages, unharmed, within the hour, or face the consequences. When no hostages were freed, an assault force retook the prison, killing thirty-nine individuals (twenty-nine inmates and ten hostages).[4]

The Attica uprising was one illustration of how institutional violence can manifest itself in a variety of forms, among them riots, other types of major disturbances, victimization of one inmate by another, staff brutality toward inmates, inmate assaults on staff, and self-inflicted violence by prisoners. Whatever form it takes, institutional violence is a severe indictment of the correctional policy of imprisonment. The more than 300 prison riots since 1970 have established the danger and the unstable character of contemporary prisons.[5] To commemorate the forty-fifth anniversary of the Attica uprising, prisoners across the country staged strikes to draw attention to a wide range of grievances, from compensation to prison conditions.

---

3. Ibid.

4. New York State Special Commission on Attica, *Attica.*

5 Nicholson, "Incarcerated Stage Nationwide Prison Labor Strike."

Accommodating the Gangs

Gangs received more than their share of blame for the prison chaos fueled by violence. But In Illinois, it was true that several supergangs—the Vice Lords, the Gangster Disciples, the Black P Stone Nation, and the Latin Kings—warred with each other and had immense control over the prison population.

In California and Illinois especially, prison wardens began to negotiate with gang leaders to maintain control of their institutions. A gang leader would go to a warden and say something such as: "There are riots in two other prisons in this state and we could have a riot here. The place is ready to explode. But if you and I can work together, I can assure you that there will not be a riot in this prison. I can even assure you that we will have few, if any, assaults of staff and few, if any, rapes of inmates. In other words, I can keep the lid on the place."

I know that such conversations took place. Inmate leaders have told me so, and wardens themselves have admitted this to me. I even had one director of a major corrections system tell me that his wardens felt they sometimes had no choice but to negotiate with gang leaders. This situation persisted for a good decade or more. And over the years, I personally benefited from this informal relationship when gang leaders were able to call my classes at the university and talk with my students. Gang leaders told me of the benefits they received at the time, including preparation of food, cell assignment, having some say over what took place at the prison, and more extensive phone calls.

Taking Back the Prison

In Illinois, the authorities' effort to take the prisons back from the gangs has occurred in stages. The first stage involved implementing unit management at Stateville.

Throughout the 1970s, Stateville, a maximum-security facility, was a disaster to manage. This overpopulated institution was controlled by violent Chicago-based prison gangs. For inmate gang members and staff at all levels, extreme stress was a fact of life. In September 1973, ten employees were taken hostage, and in January 1977, two correctional officers (lieutenants) were stabbed fatally, in separate incidents. A year later, the warden of another prison described the atmosphere at Stateville in this way: "When correctional officers leave Stateville each day, they look like they're coming out of a war zone."[6] The prison was known as a graveyard for wardens who signed on, fully realizing they would probably last no more than a year or two. The stress and pressure they experienced simply was exhausting.

Acceleration of Gang Control

Following the January 1977 stabbings, Stateville was on lockup for most of the spring. The delivery of such services as laundry, counseling, and library access was sporadic. Over the summer of 1977, gang inmates became more aggressive, confronting staff regularly. Staff members were on the defensive; they had been warned to avoid retaliatory measures toward inmates because of the further danger of being indicted for brutality.

That fall, Stateville was used as a location in the shooting of a television movie, *The Ron LeFlore Story*.[7] During the two months of filming, problems were greatly diminished, apparently because the inmates did not want to bring bad publicity upon themselves. But as soon as the film crew left, intimidation began anew.

The seriousness of the situation was evident to everyone in the Illinois Department of Corrections over the next six months. In separate incidents in July 1978, inmates locked correctional officers out of two of the round cell houses and held gang meetings there. The second lockout occurred only three days prior to a riot at the nearby Pontiac Correctional Center. It was clear to everyone in the department that the state's prisoners were out of control.

6. Interviewed by Bartollas in the 1980s in Illinois prisons.
7. *The Ron LeFlore Story* is a made-for-television movie.

The prison was on lockdown for most of the fall of 1978, but rumors had it that some gang members were freely roaming the institution. In December, after the lockdown was lifted. the inmates took over a cell house and supposedly had a party at which alcohol was available and perhaps narcotics as well.

American Correctional Association Management Plan

In January 1979, Gayle Franzen, the new director of the Illinois Department of Corrections, requested assistance for Stateville from the American Correctional Association (ACA). Representatives from the ACA visited Stateville and agreed that the prison was out of control, that necessary services were not being provided, that communication and morale problems existed among the staff, that the institution had severe problems with security, and that the facility was unclean.

The ACA then assigned a team of three individuals to develop a plan for regaining control of the prison. Two additional consultants were called in to design a system for classifying the inmates. The plan that emerged had the following objectives:

- To place the institution on deadlock (inmates locked in their cells twenty-four hours a day)
- To make significant headway on improving the cleanliness and appearance of the institution
- To address the issue of staff morale and assignment
- To reclassify the inmates and set up a system of unit management

The implementation of the plan was begun by placing the institution on lockdown and by emptying one of the housing units—B East. After the unit was thoroughly cleaned and mechanical repairs were made, inmates from each of the round cell houses were transferred to B East, where they were given fresh bedding and linens. The emptied cell houses were then thoroughly searched, using dogs to locate firearms, explosives, and narcotics.

Measures had been established to provide inmates with basic services during the lockdown.

Inmates also were classified into three groups:

Group 1. Inmates in this group were generally considered disruptive within the institution due to one or more of the following factors: aggressive and assaultive behavior during incarceration; predatory behavior, gang leadership, and/or heavy involvement in gang activities; chronic disciplinary problems involving confrontation with other staff and/or residents; and aggressive homosexual behavior.

Group 2. These inmates were expected to make an essentially normal adjustment. Though some minor disciplinary problems might be experienced, they would not normally require major disciplinary action, nor would they indicate a serious adjustment problem. Many of these individuals may have demonstrated bad behavior in the community, but they generally conformed to incarceration.

Group 3. These inmates required separation from the more institutionally sophisticated and more aggressive inmates due to their inability to cope with the pressures that might be imposed upon them. Often, these inmates were younger, physically smaller, slight of build, physically handicapped, and/or known have a history of medical problems. Inmates in this grouping may have been on voluntary lockup status or assigned to the general population at the time of the assessment. The fact that an inmate requested protective custody was not sufficient to determine placement within this group.

Execution of the Plan

Once the overall plan was approved, the logistics of implementation had to be worked out. The only staff members involved in the ACA pilot project at this point were the top administrators of Stateville. Department personnel and the ACA consultants were split into two teams; one concentrated on basic service delivery, and the other worked out a search scheme.

The delivery team had to decide what services would be provided, how frequently they would be available, and how they would actually be delivered. In designing the search procedure, the search team dealt with the following concerns: what uniform procedures with personnel would be used in the searches, how personnel from other institutions would be used, what property would be considered contraband and therefore be confiscated, and what the disposition of these items would be.

On the evening of Friday, February 22, the lockup began, with state police in the area on standby. The following morning, the first action taken by the staff was to remove ten inmates considered "heavy" gang leaders. Each was moved out of his cell and individually escorted by members of the tactical squad to police cars, for transport to the Federal Metropolitan Center in Chicago. Next, the inmates were removed from B East cell house and placed in available cells throughout the institution. After B East was cleaned, all the inmates from the first designated cell house were moved there. On this crucial day and then in successive weeks, the prisoners caused no problems. Inmates stayed in B East for three days while their cell houses were searched and cleaned.

Classification began during the final week of the lockup; all 1,950 inmates were classified in two weeks. The initial results indicated that there were 400 in Group 1, consisting of gang leaders, strong group followers, or inmates with serious behavior problems; 1,400 in Group 2, defined as normal inmates; and about 100 in Group 3, being inmates who were likely to be preyed upon. Because this breakdown was not compatible with accommodating them in six cell houses, Group 2 was then divided into two subgroups: "lights" and "heavies." A reshuffling resulted in approximately 800 inmates in Group 1, another 800 in Group 2, and 300 in Group 3. All inmates were placed in their permanent housing. Groups 2 and 3 were placed in separate cell houses, but there were Group 2 inmates in each housing unit. Inmates were not segregated in terms of education and industries programs because of the difficulty in providing separate programming for the two groups. Furthermore, it was reasoned that a Group 2 inmate could transfer out of an industries or education program if he felt too much pressure.

New staffing arrangements called for each unit to have a unit manager, a captain in charge of all security people, the casework supervisor in charge of correctional counselors, two lieutenants, four sergeants, a leisure-time activity person, a medical person, and correctional officers. All the unit managers had been selected and were functioning when the institution came off lockup on April 1.

The gangs initially laid low and kept their gang activities hidden, but they gradually began to recruit members in their new cell houses. Although there had been no serious problems since unit management was instituted in mid-1979, institutional administrators knew there were no guarantees that serious problems would not arise in the future. After all, the inmates were still the same people, staff members were still being intimidated, and prisoners were still being assaulted by other prisoners. Nevertheless, it appeared that the institution was safer now for both inmates and staff. It is significant that after unit management was instituted, only fifty inmates chose protective custody as compared to more than three hundred before the conversion. Tomorrow may be different, it was concluded, but for today, unit management had assisted in bringing order from the chaos at the Stateville Correctional Center.

Documents pertaining to this unit management reorganization at Stateville were given to me by officials of the Illinois Departments of Corrections and are discussed so extensively here for several reasons: (1) the reorganization was the first concentrated and apparently successful effort made by the department in Illinois to take back the prison from the gangs; (2) the separation of gang leaders and strong gang supporters was perceived at the time as a policy change that would be needed in the long term; and (3) the reorganization gave the department confidence that it was possible to win the battle with the gangs. What emerged in the next three decades in terms of gang control came out of this ACA reorganization plan at Stateville.

Further Steps in This Process

The fact is that officials of the Illinois Department of Corrections had to restore order in their prison facilities. What they intended to do is just what took place at Stateville—they instilled the sound, proactive leadership so essential for a humane prison. A number of significant and positive changes have resulted, and critical components have been identified. For example:

- The classification of inmates into appropriate groups not only reduced gang behavior but also improved the staff's morale and sense of safety.

- The separation of exploitative gang members received strong support from vulnerable inmates. Whatever the prison experience entails in a free and democratic society, it must provide safety for both inmates and staff.

- The provision of basic services is an absolute must in a humane prison.

- The removal of weapons from inmates is a further necessity in a humane prison.

When I was asked by staff members of the Department of Corrections at the time if I supported their reorganization strategy at Stateville, I indicated that I did, for the reasons just cited. I certainly do not see any feasible advantage in gangs being in control of the prisons.

I also believe that prison administrators cannot negotiate with gangs or their leaders. Gang leaders may promise (and seem to deliver) safety to the facility in return for having some say over what happens in their lives, and this may appear to be a way to prevent or curtail violence. But prison administrators cannot relinquish their control over the prison no matter what the justification.

Yet in spite of the changes that have taken place since the 1980s throughout the Illinois prison system. I think back on Johnnie Walton's account of Rico's experience in the system after his

1983 incarceration and still find myself somewhat troubled. "Minister Rico started to settle back into prison life," Walton recalled in a letter to me, "only this time he realized his mistakes and started to plan and organize like he was supposed to from the beginning: Could it be too late this time?" He elaborated:

> The Prison Administration came up with the "master plan" to crush all of the so-called leaders in the system, and Minister Rico, Larry Hoover, Latin King Gino, and a few others were at the top of the list. They started off with what they called "the Circuit," to keep those leaders from stopping in one place and communicating with anyone for any long period of time. One didn't know when he was going to be pulled out of his cell and shipped out when he was on the circuit, and you didn't stay in one place much more than thirty days! They also came up with a plan called "interstate compact transfers," where they transferred a leader out of state indefinitely to who knows where.
>
> They transferred inmates to [places] like Walla Walla, Washington and Tucson, Arizona, New Mexico, and other places where a black man was in the minority and the Mexicans and Indian inmates hated their guts, and wanted to kill them at every opportunity. So, the leaders in those positions such as Minister Rico and others went through a world of changes in the early 1990s.

What do we know about these organizational changes, as described by Walton? Actually, "the circuit" was a strategy that the Federal Bureau of Prisons had used for some time. The bureau would transfer troublemakers on a regular basis from one prison to another: some bureau staff called it "bus therapy." In itself, there is nothing wrong with this approach; it does, though, show the inability of the prison to maintain control without using such techniques. Rico was put on the circuit for three years, and every thirty days, he was moved to a different institution.

Clearly, there is some advantage in moving gang leaders around because it makes gang leadership more unstable and renders the leaders less able to develop strategies and means of exerting their influence. But at the same time, there is a danger of creating a power vacuum in an institution, for younger gang members who assume leadership roles may actually generate more chaos in the facility.

An example from my own experience is illustrative. I was an expert witness in a murder case in Iowa involving the facility where the prominent gang leader Willie Lloyd had been incarcerated. After Lloyd was released from the prison, the remaining Vice Lords were left in turmoil. Out of haste and confusion—and in the absence of Lloyd's leadership—they decided to commit a double homicide over situations that could have been resolved without bloodshed. When they were trying to determine who would carry out the hits on two inmates who had been chosen for retribution, a prisoner with just a month to go before his release volunteered for the job. He killed the inmates and was later convicted of the crimes; he is spending the remainder of his life in prison. The VLs never recovered from the way they handled the whole situation.

The use of the circuit was apparently terminated in 1986, but interstate compacts have been used by both state prisons and the Federal Bureau of Prisons for some time. This tactic is a means to reestablish order by getting those who are perceived as provoking disorder out of the prison. Again, in and of itself there is nothing wrong with the practice of transferring gang leaders or troublemakers to prisons in other states or in the federal prisons. The disturbing and unacceptable problem arises when inmates are transferred to facilities in which their racial background is going to create problems for them. If Walton was correct in the account he relayed in his letters, the practice comes close to torture and is barbaric and has absolutely no place in a humane prison system.

I am also bothered by two developments that are not included in the description provided by Johnnie Walton: the enactment of the no-gang-identification rule (and punishment for violation of it) and the opening up of the Tamms correctional facility in 1998, a move intended to get troublemakers out of the way by moving them into a supermax prison.

Public schools in the United States have used the no-gang-identification rule since the early 1990s. Students have been forbidden to wear gang colors, flash gang identification signs, write gang graffiti, or in any other way identify themselves with a gang. And they have faced varying types of discipline, all the way to expulsion, for violating this rule.

For the public schools, this strategy may make sense, and one might argue that it is necessary for gang-controlled prisons to adopt a similar strategy. My concern arises when inmates are thrown into segregation for violating the rule or even transferred to a supermax such as Tamms. Such punitive measures have no place in a humane prison.

Johnnie Walton, when it was identified that he was writing me about Rico's gang history, was placed in segregation and then transferred to Tamms. That facility represented a reversion to corrections of the Dark Ages: prison administrators who decided to transfer any inmates there should have had to do a year or so at Tamms themselves, being locked up twenty-four hours a day.

Indeed, whoever came up with the idea of Tamms deserves our scorn. It was bad in strategy and even worse in implementation. It was intended to brutalize inmates, who more often than not often were driven insane by the experience. In a later chapter, I will discuss Tamms and Rico's transfer there in greater detail.

Rico's Adjustment to Yet Another New Environment

Back in 1983, Rico had been returned to prison after wreaking havoc in his community for more than two years on parole. In those years on parole, he discovered a new gang environment on the streets, an environment based on the trafficking and use of drugs. Rico was a little out of step, on the one hand, in terms of adjusting to this new environment, but on the other, he was familiar with what it meant to be a thug—and he had always known how to survive.

Along with a few followers, he went on a crime spree in the community back then, forsaking all the religious tenets he had adopted in his prior incarceration. As Walton suggested, he was fortunate that he was finally arrested and returned to prison at the time he was because he probably would not have survived much longer on the streets.

But the raw fact is that he would remain in prison for nearly twenty-nine more years. It was a different prison, of course, and his role as a gang leader was diminished to some extent; furthermore, during his first three years back in confinement, he was on the circuit, so every month he was on the move. But this time around, he did not want to earn any disciplinary tickets, nor did he want to receive disciplinary segregation. Above all, he did not want to become identified as a troublemaker.

Rico had climbed back on the wagon. Now, he was determined to be a positive leader. He wanted to make an impact on the Vice Lords he met in prison so they could turn their lives around and return to the community and make something of themselves. Yet due to the no-gang-identification rules, everything he did to work toward those goals had to be done under the table. Rico's contact with other gang members, their contacts with him, their ability to function as a group, the task of maintaining discipline and control over other gang members, and the recruitment of new gang members all had to be done differently than in the past. Rico had to be careful. The next chapter will examine how he was able to function in this diminished capacity.

8

Readjustment to Prison, Leadership, and Influence on Others

A second redemptive script in Rico's life occurred when, now known as Minister Rahim, he began to exert a positive influence on inmates he encountered while he was in the penitentiary. In that period, it was not easy to accomplish this given the crackdown on gangs. As described in the prior chapter, Rico also had to deal with the circuit, whereby he was continually moved from one prison to another. What was so impressive about the beneficial influence he managed to exert is that when inmates he had contact with returned to the streets, many became law-abiding citizens and kept away from drug use and trafficking. But I am getting ahead of the story.

What I want to do here is examine leadership capacity. To that end, I will evaluate the attributes of leadership, look at what leaders attempt to communicate to their followers, and judge how successful they are in doing so.

Attributes of Leadership

The attributes of a leader are those qualities that give the person the ability to lead and influence others. In some cases, these very attributes can also result in a leader's downfall or destructiveness. Rico Johnson has a number of attributes that set him apart from others, the most significant being his resilience, command presence, persistence, thoughtfulness, intuitive nature, communication skills, and no-nonsense approach. I will examine each of these in turn to see how they have played out in Rico's life.

Resilience

We know that many of today's youths face a host of negative influences in their lives—among them substance abuse, gang affiliations, teenage pregnancy, and school violence. Despite these and other hardships, however, some young people remain resilient; that is, they are able to persevere in the face of difficulties and become productive citizens.

Rico Johnson did not display this resilience as a child or teenager. But over the span of his life, which included forty-one years in prison, his resilience eventually became apparent. And it was his resilience that resulted in his having such a positive impact on so many inmates in prison, an impact that persisted even after their release. His resilience also prevailed following his own release from prison, when he faced one obstacle after another. It was his resilience that drove him to make a difference in the lives of youths, all in an effort to keep them from becoming Rico Johnsons themselves and spending most of their lives in prison.

Underpinning Rico's resilience are a set of apparently innate characteristics that enable him to fend off or recover from life's misfortunes. Those who study resilience claim that youths thrive when (1) they live in environments that offer caring and supportive relationships, (2) they have high expectations for behavior and attitudes (for themselves and others), (3) they have opportunities to participate in a meaningful way in positive experiences, and (4) they are able to bounce back from adverse happenings. Rico especially seems to possess the final three traits: he has always had high expectations for himself and others, he has attempted to provide opportunities for others to meaningfully participate in positive experiences, and he has been able to recover from disappointing events.

Command Presence

There was no question who was in charge when Minister Rico was incarcerated with other gang members, and the same has been true ever since his release from prison. Though he seems to be quiet by nature, he still has a presence about him. When he comes into a room, that presence is immediately apparent. When he talks to a gang member in the community, this person instantly becomes aware of the presence of Minister Rico. There is a stature about him that sets him apart from others.

Persistence

Rico Johnson is one persistent person, as has been demonstrated time after time in his life. He has survived forty-one years in prison, being disappointed year after year in his appearances before the parole board. He was supposed to have eighteen years left in his sentence when he was returned to prison in 1983, but he eventually did twenty-nine.

When I participated in several of his parole hearings, I was just baffled by how hopeful he was despite being turned down for parole time after time, regardless of all the years he had served and the fact that he had no disciplinary infractions. I remember thinking, how does he get back up? I was sure he was going to leave the prison feet first, to be unceremoniously buried in a potter's field or given a family-arranged funeral in the community.

Then, instead of being released at his parole hearing in 1992, Rico was ordered to get his stuff together because he was going to be transferred to yet another prison. Rather than going home as he had hoped, he was sent to Tamms, one of the worst facilities in the nation. Until it was closed in 2012, this supermax prison routinely violated American standards of fair treatment and good mental health. Yet somehow, due to a combination of his resilience and his persistence, Rico survived his time in this horrible facility.

Communication Skills

Certainly, part of the appeal that Rico brings to the table as a leader involves his strong communication skills. Throughout his imprisonment, these skills were augmented by the fact that others looked to him as their mentor and continued to feel grateful for his guidance. They found him to be supportive of their growth and development, and as a result, he enjoyed strong loyalty from all those he interacted with during his imprisonment as well as his time in the community.

Thoughtfulness

Rico's apparently innate thoughtfulness was only enhanced by his experiences while he remained locked up. During a good number of those forty-one years, Rico was held in solitary confinement, especially when he was in the supermax prison at Tamms. As a result, he had time to read and to reflect, and he did a great deal of both. He had time to think and to sharpen his natural cognitive skills.

Intuitiveness

Rico's intuitiveness is evident in how well he reads people. Since his release in 2012, his intuitive skills have repeatedly come into play in the decisions he has made. Relatively little has been written about gang members being released from prison after serving long sentences, but we do know that police watch them very carefully. Consequently, a former inmate's intuition is key in avoiding not only criminal behavior but also everything else that in any way resembles wrongdoing.

No-Nonsense Approach

As is often seen with politicians, the powerful do not brook opposition; indeed, it has been said that if you oppose political leaders, they will crush you. Rico grew up on the streets, and he learned to be strong—that is what survival is all about. This was true during his time in prison as well, for he did not rise in the Vice Lord hierarchy by being passive or weak. One of the reasons he succeeded is because everyone knew he would take no nonsense.

Characteristics of Rico's Leadership

During his long imprisonment, Rico developed a leadership style that has been refined over the years and has been expressed most clearly since his release in 2012. Certain characteristics have distinguished him from other gang leaders, and interestingly, these actually resemble traits of highly successful leaders in the public and private arenas.

Rico Believes That He Can Make a Difference

Rico is sure he can make a difference in the lives of others. In an interview I conducted with him after his 2012 release, he answered the question of whether he had helped a lot of individuals by saying, "Yes, a great many, but I don't feel I am done." He added, "I would hope that every guy I encountered I made them a little better than they were when I met them." Because of this conviction, he continues to write to those parolees he felt he was influencing while they were incarcerated.

He noted: "I am writing to most of the young men I met in prison. I want to stay in communication with them, and I am writing to convey to them what I have experienced and how I wouldn't want them to experience the same thing. Instead, I want them to take a different road in order to develop a better lifestyle and a better direction for their lives."

In a real sense, he attempts to touch the lives of nearly everyone with whom he has contact. Rico is realistic enough to know that the playing field that matters is not the prison—it is the community that inmates rejoin after their release.

Rico Believes He Needs to Use a Hands-On Approach

Rico is an avid reader who prefers solitude, but realizes the importance of personal contact. As a result, in spite of attempts by prison administrators to reduce his contact with other inmates—which included three years on the circuit and the threat of being placed on segregation for gang-related activities—he continued to have contact with inmates whenever he could. He knew that disciplinary offenses could prevent his parole, if the state would ever grant that. Still, whenever the opportunities presented themselves, Rico would visit other inmates. He was always teaching about Allah, and he continually reminded those inmates that their lives could and should be different when they returned to the community.

Rico Believes He Must Have a Supportive Team

Rico has always been aware that, both in the community and in the prison, he must have strong support from those who are loyal to his vision of the Vice Lord's mission. Given the criminal rampage that occurred when he was released in 1980 and became a terror in the community, he now knows his support must be based on community outreach and individual transformation. Upon his release in 2012, there was some concern—both in Rico's mind and among some of his followers—about how much this supportive team would appear to be gang oriented. He was well aware that law enforcement and the courts kept a close eye on what he was doing in the community.

Rico Attempts to Model Positive Behaviors

Rico believes that before he can expect others to behave appropriately, he himself must demonstrate trustworthiness, loyalty, and commitment to what is known to be true. Moreover, as part of this modeling, Rico has tried to show Vice Lords how to interact effectively with other gang members without losing their respect and without being compromised, manipulated, or taken for a ride.

Peace Is Better Than Violence

As a youth, Rico marched with Martin Luther King Jr. but concluded that King's nonviolent approach was not something he could accept. He much preferred the way of Malcolm X, which was more focused on aggression. Certainly, Rico's crimes in the community and his struggle for leadership among the Vice Lords in the prison context reflected Malcolm X's style much more than Martin Luther King's.

Yet a change has gradually emerged in Rico's leadership style. For instance, he developed a good relationship with Larry Hoover, head of the Gangster Disciples, while they were incarcerated in the same prisons; I was always amazed at how well they got along. I also found it interesting that he never seemed to be in battles or conflicts with other gang leaders, especially in the final stages of his imprisonment. And even with the ongoing feud that pitted Willie Lloyd and the Unknown Vice Lords against Rico Johnson and the Conservative Vice Lords, Rico called Willie weekly during the last months of Lloyd's life. Equally interesting, Rico had relationships with members of other gangs, both in prison and in the community. Sam Dillon, a friend of mine and a former enforcer of the Black P Stone Nation, had a long relationship with Rico. And one Saturday morning a couple of years ago, I received a call from Rico and Wallace "Gator" Bradly, a Gangster Disciple and an advocate of Growth and Development; they were both involved in presenting a conference on peace in Minneapolis at that time.

Drugs Are a Major Stumbling Block to Working with Gangs

Rico himself has never been a drug user, though he has sold a little marijuana, especially while in the joint. But when he was released on parole in October 1980, he became acutely aware of what a major stumbling block drugs would present to any efforts to promote positive change in the community. It did not take him long to realize that drugs were where the money was, and he soon joined other drug traffickers in attempting to expand their markets and make as much money as they could. He was successful, but a considerable amount of criminal behavior was required to stay on top of the drug trade. Furthermore, it was dangerous work, and by the time he was sent back to prison in 1983, the opposing forces were closing in. His right-hand man was found dead shortly after Rico's arrest.

After he returned to his Muslim faith during the long incarceration that followed, Rico knew that in trying to influence inmates in a positive way, he was facing a stubborn mind-set. He put it this way: "They thought that the positive teachings being taught in the prisons [were] a waste of time in society. They thought that being a Muslim was being a square. If you didn't have a Cadillac, a pocket full of money, and a dope house, you [had] no value or worth."

Rico frequently references the fact that the separation of the branches in the Vice Lord Nation stemmed from the influence of the drug nation. He feels that it may be necessary to start with young Vice Lords when they first come into institutions and try to instill in them in a new level of consciousness. But he acknowledges that this is going to be a tough challenge. When they get out on the streets and have to deal with the drug business, even those who seemed to be going another way in prison all too frequently become weak willed and go after the money.

Hopefulness Is a Major Feature of Rico's Leadership

What seems to be a key to Rico's leadership is that he is fundamentally a person of hope. The scriptures of many religious traditions suggest that without hope, a person perishes. It was hope that got Rico through forty-one years of prison and enabled him to survive almost nine years in the hellhole of Tamms. It also motivated him to touch other lives while he was confined in prison, and it has propelled him to work with children and families since he was released. As a person of hope, even when he is facing the demon of drug use and trafficking Rico remains optimistic that inroads can be made.

Communication between Gang Leaders and Their Followers

Some gang leaders have developed a protocol for use in teaching their followers. Larry Hoover, for example, taught the Gangster Disciples what we now call *The Blueprint*. Convinced that what he was sharing with his members had to be documented, Hoover dictated his thoughts and had them put on paper. The manuscript was passed around to a few people (including me), who added their own input into what eventually became *The Blueprint of a New Concept*.

What Minister Rico was teaching his followers in prisons can be divided into three broad parts—beliefs and structure, religious affirmations, and practical advice.

Beliefs and Structure

Beginning in the 1960s, the Conservative Vice Lords developed a number of beliefs and practices that formed the basis of their organization, some of which were discussed in chapter 5. The Vice Lords abide by twenty-one "supreme constitutional laws," including the following: "death before dishonor," "the code of silence," "business before pleasure," and "take no shorts." In addition, the gang has fourteen "keys" and ten "commandments." Their regular meetings, usually held every week, are called "goals" and "golden gatherings."

When the gang adopted Islam in the 1970s, two concepts were heavily relied upon—the "Al-Fatiha" and the "Holy Divine," which in fact is a prayer and oath for gang members. As previously stated, the members wear black (representing race) and gold (wealth). They also have sometimes worn black capes bearing the words *Vice Lords* written in gold, as well as earrings. They tend to greet each with the slogans "All is well" and "Almighty." They refer to each other as "lord," "family," or "Joe."

Religious Affirmations

Rico stated that he taught the brothers in his gang certain concepts:

> I try to please God in all that I do. I want to please Allah. God has cleaned this up for me. He has forgiven me for my injustices. I taught all these brothers. They took lessons from me and learned from it. I used the years in prison to learn. It made me feel good.
>
> I took the opportunity to know the true man. I learned that if you get a young man before he grows bad [you can] get him involved in a positive engagement.
>
> What drove me is that they are killing themselves over nothing. The administration is watching me, and I have to move slowly.

Practical Advice

Additionally, Minister Rico had practical advice to offer those being released from prison whom he had worked with for some time; he wanted each of their lives to have a positive ending. This practical advice was expressed in interviews I conducted with a number of the men whose lives had been changed by their interactions with Minister Rico.

The main points of Rico's practical advice were to stay away from violence and drugs; to find employment; to have a stable family relationship; to take care of your children; and to remember that the police are looking over your shoulder, so be sure you give them no reason to harass you. My interviews with some of the men Minister Rico counseled elicited interesting insights, as relayed in the paragraphs that follow:

Carl O'Neill. Fifty-two at the time of our interview, Carl O'Neill said:

> I been in trouble all my life, been in jail, and because of criminal behavior, I have been in prison five or six times.
>
> I knew his [Rico's] position in the Vice Lords. He was feared by most people. I think the reason he touched me was that my life was not going anywhere. We were in Dixon together, and I saw him at least once a week.
>
> When I lost my mom, he showed me so much love. I became aware of how much he loved me. I never sold a lot of dope. I have taken a lot of it. In getting my life together, I turned to Christianity. And, we never had a problem over that. I thank God everyday he was in my life.
>
> There were times in the joint when I was ready to go crazy. He would pick me up. He did far more for me than I did for him. What is really amazing to me is that when he got out, I gave him $50, and he sent most of it back to the penitentiary.
>
> He believed that you can be anything you want to be. The administration looked upon him as a security risk. To keep him from being a security risk, they moved him around. They were always letting him know that they were watching him, but still he went out of his way to help me.
>
> He never complained. He never asked me for anything. I am now a deacon in my church.[1]

Eddie Wells. Another former inmate, Eddie Wells, spoke of how Rico influenced him:

> I actually was a cellie with him for about nine months. Rico had turned his life around. When I met him, things

---

1. Phone interview in 2013.

had begun to turn around for him. He was working on being a good citizen, family man, and concerned about children.

Rico saw something in my wife and in me. Rico talked to me and said you have a good wife. Rico was one of the first ones to make me realize what I had. For me, he established a good relationship with my wife.

When I was released, I became a born-again Christian. I became involved in the Koinonia House Ministry Community, and I see myself with a ministry of my own. You can go online and see my testimony.

Rico wants to influence everyone he possibly can. He feels responsible for some of the things going on in society. He doesn't want people to be mistreated or used. When he was incarcerated, he made sure you had all that you needed. He set a standard to be a role model. I am happy that I met him.[2]

Vincent Denny. Another former inmate, named Vincent Denny, added these remarks:

Rico has a gift. He is determined, actually one of the most determined people I've ever known. He is able to communicate and is concerned that we are able to do something for the community.

Rico says what was important to him. "I wanted others to learn and study these lessons. I kept in contact with those I had met in prison. I would hope that everyone I met I made a little better. I did not want them to go through what I had to go through." [3]

Johnnie Walton, Sr. Johnnie Walton, whose letters to me were extremely helpful in writing this biography, had this to say about Rico:

[He] had real power in the joint. His influence was so great that he was a lawman, a high sheriff. When you had a problem, you would go to Rico. He was a "Godfather"-like figure.

2. Phone interview in 2013.

3. Phone interview in 2012.

> Let me say that Rico is a remarkable man, who has overcome so much in his life, has always managed to contribute in a positive manner to the lives of other individuals. He refused to be broken by the system, and he will never give up his struggle to be free and to contribute in a meaningful way to our society. Men of his caliber and intelligence and leadership ability are desperately needed in this society.[4]

Walter A. Grey. Walter Grey, another former inmate who knew Rico (Rahim) in the joint, commented:

> Rahim is a remarkable man, who has overcome so much in his life, and yet has always managed to contribute in a positive manner to the lives of other individuals. A lifelong victim of racism, he has never himself demonstrated racist behavior. Quite the opposite, in fact. I am a fifty-four-year-old white man, who has spent the majority of his adult life in the Illinois Department of Corrections. I speak firsthand of the system and all that it has attempted to do to Rahim. He will never be broken, and he will never give up his struggle to be free and to contribute in a meaningful way to our society. Men of his caliber and intelligence and leadership ability are so desperately needed in our society.[5]

Bill Williamson. Bill "Colonel" Williamson, who was interviewed while he was coping with a terminal illness, described a different side of Minister Rico's leadership:

> There is so much to the minister's life. He is a businessman. He is well-read. The minister has always been a Vice Lord, an original Vice Lord. His word is law. When he needs stuff done, it is done. He is no one to play around with.[6]

---

4. Letter received in 2001 and interviewed in 2013.
5. Phone interview in 2013.
6. Phone interview in 2013.

Al Heronaza. Al Heronaza, one of the chaplains at the Cook County Jail and a community activist, had this to say about Minister Rico:

> Rico and I have a good relationship with one another. We have a good history and are loyal to one another. He is a giver seeking to serve hundreds and thousands of kids. He is part of my giving ministry. He picks up food and clothing, and he goes to individual homes and delivers them. We also deal with youth. We mentor them, as we bring educational and work skills to them.[7]

Chief Sundiata Kamara. Chief Kamara, a Vice Lord leader in Atlanta, contributed this statement about Rico:

> The minister has a God-given ability and charisma that, if racism had not been a factor, is such that he could have been the president or a high-ranking official. The seeds that the minister have planted, such as myself, will go on to rebuild the work of rehabilitation and education of African Americans in this country. Our goal is to make the black community an oasis for unity, brotherhood/ sisterhood, and dignity.[8]

Alonzo James. According to Alonzo James, who knew Rico in prison:

> Minister Rico is a great and awesome guy who has influenced a lot of people. He has taught me how to become involved in positive groups. What he said is that we need to avoid going the wrong way, because he went the wrong way and has done enough time for everybody. He is a good leader. He may be a small guy, but he is a hell of a thinker. He has seen it all. I have never heard him say anything wrong or negative. He is also extremely sincere.[9]

---

7. Phone interrrview in 2016.
8. Interview in October 2016.
9. Interview in September 2016.

Dr. Nehemiah Russell. Dr. Russell, an assistant principal of a Chicago high school, offered this insight:

> While in the Illinois Department of Corrections, Mr. Willie Johnson provided invaluable administration and human resources in the following 21st Century Vote and in the Gang Truce which resulted in the dramatic reduction in gang homicides rates in Chicago and elsewhere. He also supported the High School Gang Deregulation program in Englewood High School in Chicago, which was a highly effective effort of an urban high school to control gangs and make them a positive force in an urban environment.
>
> Furthermore, Rico Johnson gave support to the East Lake Management Conflict Program, which resulted in curtailing drug trafficking in Chicago. Five major housing developments were involved in this program. After being released from prison, Mr. Johnson has continued to be a positive force for change.[10]

The next chapter describes Minister Rico's struggles to be released from his long imprisonment. It was clear that the criminal justice system, especially law enforcement and the courts, did not want him back on the streets.

10. Interviewed in October 2016.

9

Discouragement, Discouragement, and Discouragement

Minister Rico had to walk a fine line as he served his time. On the one hand, he needed to avoid disciplinary offenses; he wanted to have a clean record, and for nearly twenty years, he was successful in this regard. But on the other hand, he was a recognized leader of the Vice Lords and felt he had certain leadership responsibilities, including an obligation to impact the lives of offenders who would be returning to the community.

Meanwhile, he would appear before the parole board time after time, anxiously awaiting the verdict on his own release. Following is a report from the board that was sent to Rico after his appearance in 2001.

> The basis for the Board's decision at this time is explained as follows:
>
> Inmate Willie Johnson was interviewed by the Prisoner Review Board on August 28, 2001 at the Joliet Correctional Center. All available file materials were reviewed with care.
>
> On January 19, 1983, Inmate Johnson together with his co-author forced their way into the victims' home at 609 North Lockwood, Chicago, Illinois. They tied

the victims up at gun-point and took items of personal property belonging to the victims. The victims were blindfolded, placed in a car, and carried away. The victims escaped during a police chase. Inmate Johnson and his co-author were arrested on January 20, 1983. At the time of his arrest, Inmate Johnson was on parole for a murder he committed on March 12, 1970, when he shot that victim with a revolver. Following the murder conviction, Inmate Johnson was sentenced to 25–100 years in the Department of Corrections, and was paroled on October 14, 1980. Inmate Johnson's prior criminal history includes armed robbery (1967), three counts of armed robbery (1968), an unlawful use of weapons (1969), and a parole violation, including the violation of a previous release on parole from his current sentence.

Inmate Johnson's institutional adjustment has been very satisfactory. His last disciplinary offense was received on December 1, 1995, for unauthorized property and his record during the last 5 years is described as exemplary.

He has been described as "positive," "sincere," "focused," and "determined." Inmate Johnson earned an AA degree from Lewis University. He has also acquired his GED and a barber's license. He maintains constant contact with family and friends, and his parole plans include residing in Chicago with a friend and working in her business in an administrative position. He was joined at his interview by Dr. Nehemiah Russell (friend of 30 years), Carl O'Neal (40 year old cousin), Delilah Van Pelt (60 year old sister), Dr. Clemens Bartollas (friend of 8 years), and Cathy D. Genoves (friend of five years) who made very passionate and reasoned pleas for his release on parole.

The Prisoner Review Board denies parole because there is a substantial risk that Inmate Johnson will not conform to reasonable conditions of parole, and to do otherwise would deprecate the seriousness of the offense, and promote disrespect for the law.

Parole is therefore denied.[1]

1. State of Illinois Prisoner Review Board, "Basis of Parole Decision."

Rico received similar reports after he met with the parole board each year. The frustration he felt was obvious in his remarks to me after one such hearing: "I am not in any trouble. I don't create any problems. I am not getting disciplinary tickets. What more do they want me to do?" I attended several of his parole hearings and became convinced that he would not be released in his lifetime.

I was of two minds on this issue. In one respect, I felt that it was unfair to deny him parole, because of his exemplary behavior in prison, the skills and education he had acquired there, and the viable parole plans he had developed. I felt he was being held because of the board's reluctance to return a gang member—especially a gang leader—to the streets.

But at the same time, he did have a murder conviction that had earned him a sentence of twenty-five to a hundred years. And then there was his criminal outburst that began when he was paroled in October 1980 and continued until January 1983. Given that he was involved with armed robberies and a variety of other serious crimes during those years, it apparently was deemed problematic to grant him parole.

One could argue that by the early 2000s, twenty years had elapsed since Rico was returned to prison and that a person can change a lot in twenty years. Beyond that, there were indicators that the minister had experienced genuine positive change over these years.

As it turned out, instead of seriously considering him for release the parole board shipped him to Tamms, a facility reserved for the worst inmates and troublemakers in the system. It was clear that Rico's gang involvement was pivotal in the decision issued by the Department of Corrections.

Rico's Response

I have spoken about Rico's resilience, and that resilience was apparent time after time, year after year, whenever he was denied parole. Somehow, after a brief period of mourning he would be back up, doing his time the best he could. He felt beaten down, but he was not beaten.

But Rico was shipped to Tamms. As the next chapter reports, Tamms was the type of facility that should have been left behind in the Dark Ages; it did not belong in contemporary corrections. Unfortunately, it was very effective in beating prisoners down and even destroying them. It is little wonder that inmates went mad in this grim facility.

Yet somehow, as with his parole rejections, Rico would not be broken by Tamms. Remarkably, through discouragement after discouragement, he prevailed.

So it was surprising when he was released from Tamms to the streets in August 16, 2012. He had begun to have health issues, and it simply did not appear likely that he would ever be paroled. And if he were paroled, it is important to remember that he had been locked up twenty-three hours a day for over eight years, which raises the question of how he could cope with parole life.

10

Tamms—A Nightmare

Supermax prisons appeared on the correctional scene in the 1980s. There are now more than forty states that have supermax prisons. The quality of these facilities and the nature of what takes place within their walls has varied from the very good to the very bad. Typically, inmates are locked up for twenty-three hours a day, with an hour to shower and exercise.

The Oak Park Heights Correctional Facility in Oak Park, Minnesota, is well known as a model supermax prison. Accepting their first inmates in the early 1980s, Warden Frank Wood and his committed staff operated a facility that had no escapes, no homicides among inmates, and no serious violence toward staffers. Even after Wood was promoted to the central office in the mid-1990s, eventually becoming the commissioner of corrections, the staff he had trained has continued to operate a prison in which inmates are treated with dignity and respect. In visiting this facility on several occasions, I have always been impressed that the inmates are safe and treated humanely, that their constitutional rights are respected, and that they can take advantage of productive programs. Oak Park is a supermax prison, but it is the best of the best.[1]

1. See Bartollas, *Becoming a Model Warden*.

If not the worst, the Illinois Correctional Center in Tamms, Illinois, would be in the running for this dubious distinction. In 1998, the Illinois Department of Corrections opened this facility— a prison without a yard, a cafeteria, a classroom, or a chapel. Phone calls and community activities were limited, and contact visits were not allowed. Inmates could only leave their cells to shower or to exercise alone; food was pushed through a slot in the cell door. Tamms Supermax was designed to produce sensory deprivation, and not surprisingly, the consequences of their isolation led to inmates experiencing severe depression, having hallucinations, cutting their bodies, and even committing suicide.

The first inmates at Tamms were transferred there from other prisons in Illinois so they could receive a year of shock incarceration designed to curb their disruptive behavior. Ten years later, more than a third of the inmates had been there since it opened.

Tamms had its supporters over the years. The most vocal ones were representatives of the correctional officers' union, residents of the nearby town who welcomed the well-paid jobs at Tamms, and state officials who thrived on the tough-on-crime policies implemented there.

From 2006 on, efforts were made to reform what took place at Tamms. But the prison union and legislatures representing local people fought back. Within five years, the attempted reforms were stalled, in spite of a federal court ruling that inmates at Tamms had been deprived of their due process.

The glimpses I had of the supermax prison at Tamms reminded me of the dark ages of corrections, when prisoners were brutalized and treated inhumanely. Fortunately, prison reformers in Illinois, members of the legislature, inmates' families, and the inmates themselves were able to put enough pressure on the state to close the facility. Tamms was shut down on January 4, 2013.

Minister Rico spoke about his days at Tamms:

> I thought I was going up for parole, but instead they shipped me to Tamms. They told me that I was an influential inmate who needed to be separated from the other inmates. I had not received a ticket for a disciplinary

offense for 20 years. The place was deplorable. I had a concrete slab for a mattress, a concrete desk, and a concrete toilet. If my wife and family had not supported me and visited me, I would have gone mad. The savage ways of this institution [were] so bad that you won't believe it, unless you were there.

Rico spent eight years and four months in that oppressive environment. Instead of being granted his freedom by the parole board, he had been thrown into this facility with the excuse that he was a bad influence on other inmates. The fact is that prison administrators could not find a reason to give him a disciplinary ticket, yet he had been sent on the circuit more than once—and he ended up in the hellhole known as Tamms.

While Minister Rico stayed at Tamms year after year, his diabetes was giving him trouble, he had difficulty with one of his eyes and needed surgery, and his overall health was starting to slip. It seemed likely that he would not leave the prison alive.

An Old Testament passage says that "without hope, the people perish." And at Tamms, Rico had very little reason to hope. Aside from occasional visits by his family, his existence was day after day of concrete, concrete, and concrete; given the way this facility had been designed, he was denied nearly all sensory experiences. Other inmates found various ways of coping—going mad, cutting themselves, or committing suicide—but somehow, Rico maintained a "strong mind" and was able to hang in there. How did he do it?

Recall that what had always made prison bearable for Rico was his contact with other inmates and his feeling that he was helping some of them on their journeys. These journeys would eventually take them home, and he also hoped to ease their adjustment to life on the outside. But such a journey was denied to him. Consequently, all that he had going for him was his resilience, the resilience that had supported him throughout his life. This resilience made it impossible for him to quit or to check out, regardless of how discouraged he might be. So day after day, month after month, and year after year, Minister Rico hung in there.

One of the criticisms of supermax prisons is their tendency to confine inmates for the final years of their incarceration, restricting them to a cell twenty-four hours a day. They are denied contact with others (apart from the correctional officers who take them in shackles to their showers and exercise areas). This system, based on sensory deprivation, typically fosters angry inmates who have lost whatever social skills or socialization they once had by the time they are ready for release. One might argue that this approach makes sense for the correctional system because it keeps disruptive inmates out of circulation until it is necessary to return them to their communities. But it makes no sense for society to dump these frequently hostile inmates on the streets without in any way preparing them for release.

On August 16, 2012, Minister Rico was paroled and released from prison. As will be discussed in the next chapter, he had a far different response to the community at this point than when he was paroled in October 1980. Apparently, Tamms had not done as much damage to him as it had to so many other inmates.

11

Paroled at Last

In August 2012, Willie Rico Johnson was released from Tamms Correctional Center on mandatory supervised release. When his brother-in-law Jeff picked him up at the penitentiary, Rico was delighted to be returning to his community. He settled in with his wife in Naperville, a residential area about thirty miles from downtown Chicago. He spent a quiet evening visiting with his wife's grandchildren on his first night at home.

Rico was required to wear an ankle bracelet for ninety days, since the correctional authorities did not know how his adjustment to the outside world would go. The dusty paperwork from his previous parole in 1980, which showed he was a terror in the community upon release, gave them pause, and they did not want anything of a similar nature to happen again. Also, law enforcement and court officials were well aware that returning gang leaders typically create problems because they are interfering with established networks in the community. It is not unusual for a returning gang leader to end up dead in a short period of time.

The morning after Rico's release, parole officials arrived at his house and installed his ankle monitor. On Mondays, Tuesdays, and Wednesdays, he was permitted to leave the home from 8:00

AM to 2:00 or 3:00 PM to look for a job. On the weekends, he had permission to go shopping.

Problems quickly emerged. For example, when his diabetes flared up, he needed to refill a prescription, but that was not easily accomplished. Fortunately, with intervention from his friends, the situation was resolved in short order. However, there was some concern that other health-related issues might arise and be more difficult to handle.

One of the things that brought joy to Rico was that his favorite sister's son had saved $5,000 for him to buy new clothes. Rico gave serious thought to this prospect, comparing the styles that were popular when he was locked up and the current styles. Soon enough, he was able to find some nice clothes on the racks of Chicago's stores. In addition, as the people in the streets say, you need one tailor-made suit. He did look good in his new clothes, especially in the tailor-made suit.

In the early months of his parole release, Minister Rico faced four major challenges, with many more to follow. First, he had to comply with his in-house arrest requirements. Second, he had to adjust to being home. Aside from October 1980 to January 1983, he had been in prison for forty-one years, spending his latest years in what was probably the worst supermax prison in the nation. As part of his adjustment to the outside world, he had to learn to live with his wife, for they had actually spent little time together. Third, he had to find a way to make it financially, which proved to be a daunting task. And fourth, with Bobby Gore inactive and stricken with cancer and other coleaders either retired or dead, Minister Rico had to fulfill his role as head of the Vice Lord Nation—a delicate job indeed. He had to exert leadership in a way that did not cause trouble with the men who previously had been in charge of the Conservative Vice Lords, and leaders of the other divisions of the Vice Lords had to be dealt with or at least communicated with as well.

It was not long before five leaders of the other Vice Lord gangs came around to see him. They wanted to know what his plans were and whether he was going to create problems for them.

Rico assured them that he wanted to supply solutions rather than cause problems and that he would not interfere with their operations or give them trouble.

He met almost daily with five or six inactive Conservative Vice Lords with whom he had a relationship, usually established in prison, and discussed how he could have a positive impact in the community. All of these individuals were living positive lives, and none were involved in crime. They had also distanced themselves from gangs. Significantly, active members of the Conservative Vice Lords did not attend these meetings. It was not that they they questioned Minister Rico's leadership; rather, it was that they were selling drugs and cigarettes, and they did not want or need any interference from a gang leader they really did not know.

Rico did find employment at the University of Chicago, where, as part of a federally funded program, he was paid to work with youths in the community. This job continued for over two years and ended in the spring of 2015. At that point, Rico had to depend on his wife's Social Security and the speaking fees that he received when he addressed community groups.

Before too long, he received a visit from the officials of the city township, who informed him that he was deemed an undesirable character and that it was necessary for him to move; interestingly, it was the neighbors, not the police, who wanted him to relocate. And so, Rico and his wife soon moved to another apartment, not too far from their first address. It was also in suburban Chicago, and it was as nice, if not nicer, than their prior apartment.

Rico stayed in regular contact with Bobby Gore, who, as noted earlier, was dying of cancer. In the spring of 2013, Gore passed away; he was in his seventies. Rico also kept in communication with Willie Lloyd, who now lived in Minneapolis and was disabled. The leader of the Unknown Vice Lords died in the summer of 2015 at age sixty-two.

In the late fall of 2014, Rico and his wife separated and moved to different apartments. One major problem they had faced was that Rico, having lived an isolated lifestyle for so many years, did not feel he had any space with his wife, children, and grandchildren always around their apartment.

I attended Rico's seventy-first birthday party in February 2016. Several hundred people were present at this banquet, including all levels of Conservative Vice Lords. The crowd was made up of men dressed in suits as well as low-ranking gang members wearing gold and black outfits. Minister Rico was dressed in a tailor-made tuxedo that was quite impressive. The only white person in attendance, I was wearing a sports jacket, shirt, and tie. I was not overdressed.

The cost of the banquet was $40 per person, but I was able to get in for free. We were served a meal and heard several speeches, one delivered by Minister Rico himself. Seated at the head table was Thomas Jefferson, known as the Godfather.

In the next chapter, I will examine how Rico, or Rahim, has tried to make a difference in the lives of those with whom he has come in contact, especially young people. It is more difficult to identify those whom he has touched, but it would appear to be a sizable group. He has certainly spoken to large groups and his programs for youth have attracted sizable numbers of young people.

12

A Godfather in Action

The "godfather" title is derived from organized crime, especially the Italian mafia. So well depicted on the big screen in *The Godfather*, the mafia is traditionally a strong hierarchy, somewhat influenced by the organization of the Roman army. In this model of leadership, a don, or godfather, rarely issues orders directly to the workers who will carry them out but instead passes instructions down through a chain of command. This approach insulates the higher levels of the organization from law enforcement if the lower-level members who actually commit the crimes are captured or investigated.

The godfather in an organized crime family has several roles:

1. He controls the organization, and his orders cannot be questioned; they must be obeyed.

2. He provides for his organized crime family; at times, this entails securing food or other necessary goods.

3. He must watch out for and protect his family from opposing organized crime groups or gangs.

4. He is responsible for maintaining peace, if at all possible, with other organized crime families.

5. He provides counsel and direction for members of his family who face personal conflict, indebtedness, domestic abuse, and similar dilemmas; he also expects their compliance in carrying out his advice.

Previous Godfather of the Chicago Gangs

Thomas Jefferson was in prison in 1975 when he was given the title of godfather by Larry Hoover, the emerging head of the Gangster Disciples. The Latin Kings also looked upon Jefferson as a godfather. Formerly the leader of the Bonnie Blacks, Jefferson had influence both in the Cook County Jail and in prisons of the Illinois Department of Corrections. Even Warden Clarence Richard English, head of the Cook County Jail, acknowledged his influence. It did not hurt that he had money from previous armed robberies and that he would give funds to inmates for their various needs.[1]

Jefferson was in and out of prison for forty years and was finally released in 1989. In the 1990s, he played a dominant role in Nehemiah Russell's Englewood Gang Deactivation Program and in the 21st Century Vote, a program designed to sign up voters in minority communities. In 2016, now in his nineties, the Godfather still attended gang functions and was given recognition by all the major gangs.

Minister Rico as a Godfather

Minister Rico has been out of prison since August 2012. In many ways, his hands are tied because if he does anything that even appears improper or illegal, law enforcement officials will quickly haul him back into the justice system, returning him to a prison where he would spend the remainder of his life.

Yet he continues to be a godfather to his gang because he has great influence and power and fulfills the following vital roles:

1. Dr. Nehemiah Russell contributed this information on Jefferson in a series of phone interviews in March 2014.

1. He has been an advocate for establishing "save the children" programs ever since he was released in 2012. He has been able to get funding for this effort and find sports heroes who are willing to be involved. Through his auspices, recreational programs and instruction have been provided for the children. Rico has also given talks to young people, promoting the message that they need to stay out of trouble and not end up like he did, spending forty-one years in prison.

2. He provides crucial outreach to the community. One strong emphasis, typical of the social outreach programs the Vice Lords have conducted in the past, involves feeding local families. Minister Rico has succeeded in finding sources who donate a great deal of groceries. Vice Lords put these groceries into boxes and deliver the food to about 150 families.

3. He serves as a mentor and confidant and makes himself available to his community nearly every day of the year. Minister Rico receives phone calls and responds to the needs of those who contact him. He generally takes a low-key approach, using kindness and giving helpful advice; when needed, however, he can be firm and even confrontational. For instance, he told one Vice Lord who was in a messy relationship: "You have two women on a line, and it is not working out. They are not happy and are taking all your time to deal with them. You have to choose one or the other or drop both of them."

4. He inspires others. Minister Rico's dedication to helping others started out in the penitentiary when he encouraged an inmate to go home, stay away from crime and drugs, be a good husband and father, and live a constructive life. This dedication continues to the present day. He may not be having the success with young Vice Lords that he once did in the penitentiary, but he continues to do all he can to impact young lives.

He also helps community members find meaningful employment. When I attended Rico's seventy-first birthday party in

February 2016, I observed that the weekend event was constructed around a number of job seminars for both youths and adults.

As the Vice Lords' godfather, Minister Rico expects obedience and compliance. He may be limited in what he can do, but he remains their leader. He does not brook opposition.

Rico summarized what he is attempting to in the following statement:

> My concern is to raise the consciousness of youth. I once led them astray, but now I want to lead them to a righteous path. My intent is to give them a better chance in their life, rather than raping, robbing, abusing each other, and other members of society.
>
> It is my hope that in five years I can change the direction that many youth are going, so they can be good citizens and make something of themselves rather than be a problem.
>
> If you are not the solution, you are the problem. My hope is to give a young man and a young girl hope for the future. It is easy as hell to get into mischief, but it is hard as hell to get out. I thought it was a phase when I got into trouble, but forty-five years later I am still getting out of the hole.
>
> It is my task to help the youth to prevent the same mistakes that I made. I do have a double standard, in that I have to be very careful what I do, where I do it, and how I do it. I have to be the best I can with the tools I have to use. If I am not careful, they will have me back in the penitentiary for inciting some form of gang organization.
>
> It does look encouraging. It is slowly developing. I am trying my best to make it possible to see a positive result. At the present, I want to make sure I am focusing my talks to the right people, at the right time, and the right place. I am getting ready now to give another talk this afternoon to a group of youth.

One member of the Vice Lords recently sent me a statement that offers valuable insights into Rico's role and contribution as the godfather of his group:

After the founder or head of an organization has passed on, or moved on, the last of the heads becomes the God-father. But to most of the Vice Lord Nation, Minister Rico was always the Godfather. The *American Heritage College Dictionary* defines a godfather as "a man who sponsors a person, as at baptism (slang). The leader of the organized crime family." But in the black community, Minister Rico is looked upon as a man who for over forty years has read and studied many books and has looked at the cause and solution to many problems in his community.

Because of his experience, the black community from whence he comes calls Minister Rico a man of wisdom and discernment. This includes the older and new Vice Lords, so "the Godfather," that's what Minister Rico is according to the streets of the black community. Without mincing words, he brings peace out of chaos, sense out of nonsense; he brings direction on how to better yourself; and when he speaks, you listen because he doesn't believe in saying it twice. That's respect for who Minister Rico is and has become.

I was told of an incident by a young man who witnessed this episode firsthand but didn't want his name mentioned. When Minister Rico and a few other friends were walking down the street on 16th, which is on the west side of Chicago, Minister Rico saw a mother pleading and screaming with ten young men who were beating and stomping her son on the ground in front of her home, and worst of all in front of her family. But when Rico got there he broke it up. The young men who had beat the boy told Rico why they had done it, and Rico responded, "I don't give a damn, you better not touch him again or anyone in his family." I'll tell you this, every week someone out of that group brought money over to that boy's mother to pay for his doctor bill until Minister Rico said it was enough. Here is a man, Minister Rico, who could have said "Take care of me" but chose to say "Repay that family for the trouble you caused them." Minister Rico gave that mother back her dignity and respect in the community because everyone knew she now has a relationship with the Godfather. Talk about being selfless.

During the 2017 Christmas season, a lady with four kids came to Minister Rico and told him her story. She lost her new job where she had worked for a month because she had to go to the hospital to have a small surgery. When she returned back to work she was told she was fired and there was nothing to talk about. She said to Minister Rico with tears in her eyes, "I'm looking for nothing for myself. I just wanted to give my kids something for Christmas." She also made it clear there was no man in her children's life. Now keep this in mind: Minister Rico was still trying to put his own life back together. Minister Rico made a call and within an hour he told her where to go and pick up two $250 gift cards. To a person with nothing, that's a big deal.

Another story goes like this. During one of the holiday seasons, Minister Rico was in a restaurant where he would eat and meet with people everyday who needed his advice, his counsel, and where you got all the gossip news of what was happening in the streets. What I found astonishing was some of the old gang members who were getting paid from funding to help stop the violence in the black community actually came to Rico for his wisdom to disarm some situations dealing with the gangs that were at war with each other. Back to what I was saying earlier . . . Minister Rico on this particular day was listening to a person who was president of a not-for-profit organization; he said to Minister Rico how few turkeys and food they would be giving out this year, and Minister Rico said, "Oh yeah? Well why don't all of you not-for-profit organizations and churches come together and have a big giveaway for all the people who are in need?" But the guy said most of the churches and organizations just don't get along. Minister Rico said, "Well this time they better start." So, the Minister called a meeting with as many churches and not-for-profits as he could and told them they better put away their differences and come together for this community because "this is not about any of you, it's about the community. In case each of you have forgotten." There are a few wards that make up the black community on the west side. Not only did Minister Rico bring them together for that holiday, he also got some of the gangs to go buy turkeys, chickens and ducks.

There are so many stories about the things Minister Rico has done for people. I asked Minister Rico, "How is it that you don't talk about them or take your credit for them?" Minister Rico said, "Oh yeah, huh, take credit, huh. It's not mine to take credit, to God be the glory!"

13

Some Questions to Ponder

In this concluding chapter, I will attempt to put the problem of gangs in the context of American society by addressing four key questions. First, what are the main problems that gangs bring to US society? Second, why is it difficult to walk away from gang activity? Third, what are hopeful signs in terms of gang control? And fourth, in what ways have Rico Johnson and the example of his life helped or hindered the gang problem in the United States, particularly in Illinois?

Gangs and Problems of US Society

Gangs bring problems with violence, the destruction of community life, the use and sale of drugs, and escalating rates of criminality.

Gangs Promote Violence in Our Society

Statistics track how much gang violence occurs in Chicago, and it appears to be have been increasing since 2016. It is not difficult to understand why gangs are involved in so much violence: numerous factors contribute to this harsh reality, including the culture of violence that gang youths have been exposed to all their lives, the incessant warring over drug distribution and use, the availability of weapons, and the devaluation of human life.

I was particularly struck by the shooting death of an eight-year-old youngster whose father was a gangbanger; the boy was killed by a bullet intended for his dad. I have interviewed the child's uncle, a man who turned his life around after Rico worked with him while he was doing time. The uncle had returned to the community and not been involved in gangs or drugs for the past twenty years.

Gangs across the nation have periodically attempted to reduce or eliminate violence in their communities. In fact, it is not unusual for weeks or even several months to go by without any violent incidents in a given area. But inevitably, it seems, violence erupts once more and soon returns to former levels.[1]

- The day before the 1992 Los Angeles riots, African American street gangs in the Watts neighborhood, especially the Bloods and Crips, declared a truce in a war that had killed hundreds of young men. Jim Brown, the former football star, facilitated meetings through his Amer-I-Can gang-intervention program. Across Los Angeles, other African American and Latino gangs forged cease-fires of their own, but the truce was strongest in Watts. This truce appeared to last a number of years before it faded away. Part of the reason that the truce ended is that a younger generation of gangbangers declined to participate in it.

- Unity in Peace, one of the most impressive efforts in violence prevention, was launched in the 1990s. It was supposed to be a nationwide endeavor but seemed to be more focused in the Midwest. As part of this effort, numerous national conferences were held, sometimes attended by several thousand gang members and their supporters. The testimonies offered at these conferences were inspirational. Unfortunately, however, the nationwide commitments, ranging from Los Angeles to New York, evaporated in a few years. Some concluded

---

1. See Muhammad and Muhammad, "What Happened to Gang Peace."

at the time that violence as a problem generated by gangs would persist as long as there were drugs to sell and buyers eager to consume them.

- In 2016, gangs in Baltimore—especially the Crips, the Bloods, and the Black Gangsters Disciples—called a truce during the Freddie Gray protests. So did gangs in Raleigh, North Carolina, chiefly the Bloods and Crips. And over the Labor Day holiday, gangs in Chicago declared a truce as well, but sadly it only lasted through part of the weekend.

Minister Rico was locked up during the 1990s, but he strongly supported the Unity in Peace effort, and the Vice Lords, especially Samuel Sharif Willis, were heavily involved in the Unity in Peace conferences. Yet, as history shows, truces come and go, and in the meanwhile, gang violence remains a serious and perplexing problem across the American landscape. As suggested by this biography, several critical factors make the elimination or reduction of the violence a huge challenge, among them the trafficking of drugs, the ready availability of weapons, the mixed commitment to truces by various gangs (for instance, the African Americans may support a truce but not their Hispanic or Asian counterparts), and the fact that gang members have long memories of associates who were slain by their rivals. It does not take much for a truce to falter when an episode of violence flares up.

Gangs Are Destructive to the Community,
Bringing Chaos on All Levels

In the late 1960s, the Vice Lords and the Blackstone Rangers attempted to develop outreach programs to revitalize their communities. The programs introduced by the Vice Lords between 1967 and 1970 were particularly impressive and promising. By the end of the sixties, however, due to problems stemming from the misappropriation of funds, these programs dried up.

Such problems notwithstanding, the Vice Lords have continued the quest for outreach programs throughout their history.

Bobby Gore, following his release from his false imprisonment, emphasized this goal through the remainder of his life, and Rico, ever since his release in 2012, has attempted to bring positive programs to the community as well. The reality is that gangs and their leaders need to be relentless in pursuing the means to impact their communities in positive ways.

Another Valid Criticism Is That Drug Use and Trafficking Make It Impossible to Talk about the Reduction of Violence or Effective Community Outreach Programs

The hard and stubborn truth is that drug use and trafficking limit whatever positive contributions gangs can make to society. In talking with Larry Hoover, the legendary leader of the Gangster Disciples, I asked what would happen if he simply directed the Disciples to put away the drugs. He responded without hesitation, "They would not do it." He added that if he were to propose something like that, he would lose whatever power he had over this gang.

One explanation for this sad state of affairs is that employment for minority males is an enormous problem in urban settings. A sizable number of youths and men are unable to find work, especially anything beyond minimum-wage jobs. And for many men, the dilemma is only exacerbated by the pressure of supporting wives and children. What are they to do, particularly if they have dropped out of school? Unless there is a major push to meet this problem of unemployment, drug distribution will continue to be widespread.

Drugs serve many functions for the gang member beyond the economic value derived from their distribution. For example, they are a source of collegiality and connection, and they enable people to self-medicate. Trying to curtail or stop your drug use is especially tough when all your social contacts use these substances. Underlying it all is the reality that life in the ghetto is very bleak, so bleak that it makes sense for people who are suffering to seek a measure of release, if only through chemical highs. And as we read daily, drug addiction is extremely difficult to overcome, and abstinence from drugs is exceedingly hard to sustain. Sometimes, it does not take much of a bump in the road for a person attempting to beat an addiction to resume the use of drugs.

Nonetheless, many people have succeeded in getting out of this drug trap, and they can serve as models for others in the community. Better yet, if there are solid programs and opportunities for training and mentorships in the community, many youths may not resort to substance abuse in the first place. Establishing such programs may require a political solution based on a widespread commitment to all members of our society.

High Rates of Criminality Among Members

All the research reveals that gang involvement is directly related to increased criminality for both males and females, as evidenced in Rico's early years. The relationship between violence, drugs, and all sorts of crimes makes it clear that the more involved an individual is with gangs, the more likely that he or she will be involed in criminality.

It Is Hard to Leave a Gang

Exiting from gangs is difficult, especially for those young members who do not seem to have any viable alternatives.

Youths who become involved with gangs have a closed social world. They generally are not receptive to school, to community programs, or to the guidance of their parents. The gang becomes their focus, and especially early on, they see the gang as their family and way of life.

Over and over, Rico's mother begged her son to change his life; to do something constructive; and to stay away from gangs, crime, and prison. Rico always responded that he would like to change, but it was just not feasible at the time. In those days, he did not see his life lining up in a way that could be turned in a positive direction.

For youngsters caught up in gangs today, programs such as those sponsored by the Oregon Youth Authority, described in a book by Lonnie Jackson entitled *Gangbusters,* offer positive options that communities across the country might adopt.

Young Urban Gang Members May Be a Lost Cause

In writing this book and interviewing other gang members, I came to understand that youths who are attracted to urban gangs find it difficult to see any alternatives beyond their current commitment. This is particularly true for urban youths who have dropped out of school. They see few options going forward. They fatalistically accept that they will continue on their present course until they are either killed or given a long prison sentence.

Yet with a strong policy commitment to education, job-training programs, and early childhood intervention, many youths can be saved and their communities made better places. The Safer Foundation is on the right path in the work it does to help many ex-felons find a legal path to employment in jobs that will allow them to live with their families with their dignity intact.

Hopeful Signs of Gaining Control over Gangs

Among the hopeful signs for the future are the growing numbers of gang leaders who, like Rico, seek to exert a positive influence on the gangs and their communities. Similarly, individuals and organizations outside the gang structure are more and more active in providing opportunities and positive guidance as well.

Bobby Gore, a Remarkable Leader of the Vice Lords

After being actively involved in the Vice Lords' community outreach programs in the late 1960s, Bobby Gore was wrongly incarcerated and spent eleven years in prison. During his incarceration, he spearheaded the involvement of Vice Lords in educational programs. And after his release from prison, he dedicated the remainder of his life to encouraging Vice Lords to turn away from crime.

I had the opportunity to visit with Gore in person, to write to him, and to talk with him over the phone. He also spoke to many college classes. For one of my books on juvenile justice, he provided the following statement:

> The road to success is a hard one. It begins in the family unit. It is in the family that parents plant the seeds for a young person to succeed. This young person is taught morals and ethics and learns behavior patterns.
>
> By the age of eight or nine, this young person has learned whether he will be loved, whether his needs will be met, and how fair life is. What he thinks about will have an effect on his behavior. If he feels he is on the short end of the stick, he may wake up angry as hell in the morning. He will seek elsewhere to have his needs met. He is not in a good place to compete with peer pressure.
>
> It is not long before he is in groups, doing drugs, and hurting people. It is also not long before he is serving time in the joint. When he comes out, it is even harder to achieve success. It is a lot easier to go back to crime than to stay away from it.
>
> For those of us who are determined not to go back to a life of crime, we may make it. It takes determination! It takes the opportunity to stand on your own two feet. It takes support from others. It takes luck. But, we are never out of the woods because it is real easy to go back.
>
> What I am saying is that if we want to deal with youth crime, adult crime, and street gangs, we must go back to the family unit, must improve our schools, must make our neighborhoods more desirable, and must provide other alternatives to gangs and drugs.[2]

Bobby Gore died in the spring of 2014. His advice, however, lives on: it is still very pertinent and should be heeded.

---

2. Clemens Bartollas and Stuart J. Miller, *Juvenile Justice in America*, 8th ed. (Upper Sadle Brooks, NJ: Pearson, 2017), 277.

Stories of Healing

One of the exciting things about writing a book like is this interviewing individuals who have personally experienced healing in their lives. Their stories demonstrate that people can change, that individuals can turn their lives from a negative to a positive direction, and that hope is present even in seemingly hopeless cases.

Much as David Dawley did while working with the Vice Lords, individuals may be trained to help gang leaders focus their talents and energies in noncriminal directions and achieve greater respect in the larger community. On December 21, 2016, Assistant US Attorney General Karol V. Mason described some efforts of this type:

> At the front end, initiatives like the National Forum on Youth Violence Prevention—one of the major efforts under My Brother's Keeper—are intended to reduce the number of people who enter the system. The Forum enables cities to design evidence-based, community-driven programs that create supportive environments for young people and counter their exposure to violence. Our site in Boston brought together police, youth and faith-based organizations to create a group of trained violence interrupters to mediate volatile street encounters. The city saw a 25 percent decrease in homicides between 2014 and 2015, its largest decline in sixteen years.[3]

Clearly, some programs do succeed. It requires continuous efforts by committed individuals who receive sufficient resources.

Those Who Are Committed to Working with Gangs

One of the most remarkable and influential people who has ever worked in gang intervention is a man known as Father Greg. Greg Boyle was born in Los Angeles, one of eight children, and after

---

3. National Forum on Youth Violence Prevention, ojp.gov/news/com/youthviolenceforum.

graduating from high school there, he decided to become a Jesuit and was ordained a priest in 1984.

While he was a priest in a small congregation at Dolores Mission Church, Father Greg and the local community developed positive alternatives to gang membership, including establishing a day care program and an elementary school and finding legitimate employment for youths.

In 1982 as a response to civil unrest in Los Angeles, Father Greg launched the first of gang related businesses, Homeboy Bakery. One of its purposes was to enable rival gang members to work side by side. The success of the bakery laid the groundwork for the other businesses that followed.

Father Greg is a nationally renowned speaker, and in 2005, he was a featured speaker at the White House Conference on Youth, at the personal invitation of First Lady Laura Bush. In addition to serving on innumerable committees, he has received much recognition and many awards, including the California Peace Prize, on behalf of Homeboy Industries and for his work with former gang members. In 2008, he received the Civic Medal of Honor from the Los Angeles Chamber of Commerce. Two years later, he published *Tattoos on the Heart: The Power of Boundless Compassion,* recalling his twenty-some years in the barrio of Los Angeles. Father Greg, like others across the nation, is attempting to make a difference by giving gang youths hope and providing a means of support for them so they can someday walk away from gang life.[4]

Another group with a vision is the Institute for the Study and Practice of Nonviolence (ISPN). Its mission is to teach, by word and example, the principles and practices of nonviolence and to foster a community that addresses potentially violent situations with nonviolent solutions.

This institute was founded by Sister Ann Keefe and Father Ray Malm in 2001 in the rectory of St. Michael's Church in South Providence, Rhode Island. They were distressed about the overwhelming number of young people they had to bury because of gang violence, and they decided to do something about it. They

4. Morrow, "Jesuit Greg Boyle, Gang Priest."

chose to use the principles and practices inherent in Dr. Martin Luther King Jr.'s theory of nonviolence; in the process of doing so, ISPN was born. Their dream was to teach nonviolence to everyone they could reach and to enhance people's ability to see alternatives to potentially violent solutions.

Their seemingly impossible dream has been realized, and the services they provide have expanded. Today, they offer comprehensive and holistic programs and services to support violence-prone communities and countless victims of violence. Their programs address topics such as employment and education, victim support, and streetworker outreach and reentry, and they also conduct nonviolence training and nonviolent conflict resolution workshops. Such services give clients a continuum of care to ensure that they stay alive, live with a sense of purpose, and are able to be productive members of the community.

This nationally recognized model of violence reduction is being deployed across the country in places such as Providence, Pawtucket, and Central Falls, Rhode Island; New Bedford, Fall River, and Brockton, Massachusetts; Wyandanch, New York; and Chicago. Teny Gross, ISPN's former executive director, currently occupies the same position with the Institute for Nonviolence–Chicago and is using the violence reduction model in the city's Austin neighborhood. In interviews I and a colleague conducted in 2016, gang members communicated how important Teny Gross had been in their lives. The power of his acceptance and understanding brought them to the point that nonviolence became a real possibility in their world.[5]

Willie Rico Johnson and the Gang Problem in America

American society is filled with angry people. Many feel oppressed, victimized, and isolated. Violence is freely accepted, and so is the wide use of drugs and alcohol. Nor is corruption or greed left out, as both are found at all levels in our social order. To be sure, we do

5. Web page of the Institute of the Study and Practice of Non-Violence, *Mission and Vision: Choose Peace*, 2017.

have a problem with gangs, but it is a symptom of larger problems that are rampant in our society.

Willie Rico Johnson, also known as Minister Rico and Rahim, is one of the few legendary gang leaders alive today. In fact, he is the only one at the time of writing who is not in prison. With the passing from the scene of the legendary leaders, there is likely to be instability and greater chaos in the gangs. To put it in another way, it is possible that gangs will become more violent in the future. In fact, it could be that the death of gang leaders in recent years and the absence of leadership that ensued have been major factors in the increase in violence among gangs in Chicago.

This biography of the leader of the Vice Lords has underscored several pivotal points:

1. Redemption is a key concept in the de-escalation of gangs.

2. It is possible for gang members to change and become positive forces in the community.

3. Redemption entails a number of processes, including having repentance, doing good, getting support, failing, and maturing and growing.

4. Street gangs can be active participants in social action in the community, as evident in the history of the Vice Lords and their leaders, including Minister Rico.

5. For gangs themselves to become a redemptive force, the use and sale of drugs must be greatly diminished or terminated.

6. If drug trafficking is to be eliminated or substantially reduced, it must be replaced with widespread opportunities for gainful employment. If youths do not have jobs, they will sell drugs. And if young men become adults and do not have jobs, they will continue to affiliate with gangs and be involved in trafficking drugs.

7. It is extremely difficult to leave the gang life—but it is not impossible to do so.

8. If change is to come to urban communities, it must be spearheaded by those involved in committing violent and drug crime, including gangs.

9. The gang culture is a different world. It has its own norms and values regarding what is and is not acceptable.

In sum, the prevention and control of gangs is one of the important concerns of community leaders across the nation. What presently seems to receive greater emphasis is law enforcement's repression of gangs. Unquestionably, repression can be used to prevent and control gangs in the short run, but in the long run, repression simply has not worked in getting tough on crime or the war on drugs. Nor is there any greater reason to believe that a war on gangs would have greater success.

References

Books

Bartollas, Clemens. *Becoming a Model Warden: Striving for Excellence*. Lanham, MD: American Correctional Association, 2004.

———. *A Model of Correctional Leadership: The Career of Norman Carlson*. Alexandria, VA: American Correctional Association, 2011.

Bartollas, Clemens, and Stuart J. Miller. *Juvenile Justice in America*. 8th ed. Englewood Cliffs, NJ: Pearson, 2017.

Binder, Sue. *Bodies in Beds: Privatized Prisons*. New York: Algora, 2017.

Dawley, David. *A Nation of Lords: The Autobiography of the Vice Lords*. 2nd ed. Prospect Heights, IL: Waveland, 1992.

Gore, Bobby. *The Only White Vice Lord*. Reprinted in David Dawley, *A Nation of Lords*, 2nd ed. Prospect Heights, IL: Waveland, 1992.

Jackson, Lonnie. *Gangbusters: Strategies for Prevention and Intervention*. Lanham, MD: American Correctional Association, 1998.

Keiser, R. Lincoln. *Warriors of the Street*. Belmont, CA: Cengage, 2008.

Knox, George W., and Andrew V. Papachristos. *The Vice Lords: A Gang Profile Analysis*. Chicago: New Chicago School Press, 2002.

Articles

Amoruso, David. "Chicago Vice Lord Nation Gang Boss Dead at 64." *Gorilla Convict*, July 23, 2015. http://www.gorillaconvict.com/2015/07/chicago-vice-lord-nation-gang-boss-dead-at-64/.

Bartollas, Clemens. "I Grew Up in New Orleans." In *Voices of Delinquency*, edited by Clemens Bartollas, 30–31. Englewood Cliffs, NJ: Pearson, 2008.

Campbell, Jerome. "Searching for Redemption, A Former Gang Member Struggles to Outrun His Past." *Los Angeles Times*, December 25, 2016.

http://www.latimes.com/local/california/la-me-melvin-20161225-story.
html.

Chicago Crime Scenes Project. "Conservative Vice Lords, Inc." July 40, 2009.

Conservative Vice Lords. http://chicagogangs.org/index.php?pr=CVL.

Duncan, Ian, Kevin Rector, and Scott Calvert. "The Black Guerrilla Family
Turned Baltimore Jail into a 'Stronghold,' Investigators Say." *Baltimore
Sun*, April 28, 2016. http://www.baltimoresun.com/news/maryland/.

Flood, Brian. "Former Gang Leader, Supporters Fight to Clear Name." http://
gangresearch/net/cvl/bobby.gore/goreuic2.htm.

Focal   Concerns.   https://www.newikis.com/en/wiki/Focal_concerns_
theoryNewikis.

Fountain, John W. "A West Side Story: From Crime King to Mentor." *New York
Times*, April 28, 2003.

Frank, James, Cody Stoddard, Robin Engel, and Stephen Haas. "Through the
Court's Eyes: A New Look at Focal Concerns Theory." Paper presented at
the annual meeting of the American Society of Criminology, Los Angeles,
November 1, 2006. http://www.allacademic.com/meta/p127319_index.
html.

Gore, Bobby. "The African Lion Roars." http://gangresearch.net/cvl/
evlhistoryfinal/aflion.html.

———. "The Conservative Vice Lords of the 1960s." http://gangresearch.net/
ChicagoGangs/vicelords/Gore.htm.

———. "Tell Them What We Did!" Letter to David Dawley, May 19, 1973.

Heinzmann, David. "As Chicago Killings Surge, the Unsolved Cases Pile Up."
Chicago Tribune, September 9, 2016.

IMVU   GROUPS.   http://www.imvu.com/groups/group/
A%252546V%252546L%252546N/.17.

Keegan, Anne. "Death of the Vice Lords: Chicago's Most Wanted and Feared
Gang Went Out without a Bang." *Chicago Tribune*, May 15, 1994. articles.
chicagotribune.com/1994-05-15/features/9405150490_1_gang.

Knox, George. "The Vice Lords: Aspects of and Formal and Informal Social
Organizational Life in a Gang." National Gang Information Center. http://
www.Ngcrc.Com/Ngcrc/Viceprof.Htm.

Lee, Bennie. "Former Vice Lord Leader Bennie Lee Speaks on the Vice Lords
since the Sixties." http://gangresearch.net/ChicagoGangs/vice/lords//
believeitornot.htm.

Martin Luther King and the Conservative Vice Lords. http:gangresearch.net/
cvlhistoryfinal/mlk.htm.

Maruna, Shadd. "Making Good: How Ex-convicts Reform and Rebuild Their
Lives." Washington, DC: American Psychological Association, 2001, xix.
http://dx.doi.org/10.1037/10430-000.

———. "Redemption Scrips and Desistance." In *Encyclopedia of Criminological
Theory*, edited by Francis T. Cullen and Pamela Wilcox. Thousand Oaks,
CA: Sage, 2010.

Morrow, Carol Ann. "Jesuit Greg Boyle, Gang Priest. *St. Anthony Messenger*, http://www.americancatholic.org/Messenger/Aug1999/feature1.asp.

Muhammad, Richard B., and Charlene Muhammad. "What Happened to Gang Peace." *Final Call*, May 17, 2012. http://www.finalcall.com/artman/publish/national_news_2/article_8843.shtml.

New York State Special Commission on Attica. *Attica: The Official Report of the New York State Special Commission on Attica.* New York: Bantam, 1972. OCLC 601935. http://www.nysl.nysed.gov/mssc/attica/atticareport.pdf.

Nicholson, Lucy. "Incarcerated Stage Nationwide Prison Labor Strike 45 Years after 1971 Attica Riot." September 12, 2016. https://www.rt.com/usa/358870-prison-protests-work-strike/.

Palazzolo, Joe, and John Emshwiller. "Prisoners Stage Coordinated Strikes in Several States: Inmates Protest for Improvements in Pay and Living Conditions in Demonstration Organized around 45th Anniversary of Attica Uprising." *Wall Street Journal*, September 14, 2016. http://www.wsj.com/articles/prisoners-stage-coordinated-strikes-in-several-states-1473895389.

Patel, Vikram. "Ex-Con Speaks on Gang Experience: After Serving 11 years, Bobby Gore Speaks on Current Fight for Clemency." *Chicago Flame*, March 29, 2005.

Pick, Grant. "Once a Gangbanger, Now Hal Baskin Is a "Gang Deactivator," a Peace Broker, a Role Model, and a Candidate." *Chicago Reader*, June 1994, People issue 2016. http://www.chicagoreader.com/chicago/once-a-gangbanger/Content?oid=884710.

Trigger, Modal. "Son of Gang Leader Killed as Gun Violence Rises in Chicago." Associated Press, July 6, 2015.

"Untold Story of the Vice Lords." October 13, 2013. http://thamovement1.blogspot.com/2013/10/the-untold-story-of-vice-lords-nov-1.html.

"Vice Lords and Conservative Vice Lords." Stone Grease. http://www.stonegreasers.com/greaser/vicelords.html.

"Willie Lloyd—Drug Dealer." Biography.com. www.biography-com/people/willielloyd-504960.

Correspondence

Bartollas, Clem. Letters to prison administrators in Illinois concerning Rico Johnson.

Johnson, Willie Rico [Minister Rico]. Letters through the years.

State of Illinois Prisoner Review Board. "Basis of Parole Decision for Willie Johnson." September 6, 2001.

Walton, Johnnie, Jr. Letters providing a history of Rico Johnson's life, struggles with the criminal justice system, and rise in the leadership of the Vice Lords.

Interviews

Community outreach individuals' interviews with those who had worked with Minister Rico in community projects.

Gang members' interviews with those who had known Rico Johnson in the penitentiary and the community between 2012 and 2016.

Johnson, Willie Rico. Videotaped interviews of September 2012.

Other

Beall, DeWitt. "*Lord Thing: A Chicago Street Gang Tries to Go Straight*—1970 Documentary Recalls the Doomed Reform of the Conservative Vice Lords." Chicago Reader.com. 2016. By J.R. Jones @Jr_Jones http://www.chicagoreader.com/chicago/lord-thing-movie-dewitt-beall-documentary-film/Content?oid=14438887.

Mason, Karol V., Assistant Attorney General. US Department of Justice, Office of Justice Programs. "The Road to Justice Reform." December 21, 2016. http://ojp.gov/ojpblog/road-to-justice-reform.htm?ed2f26df2d9c416fbdd ddd2330a778c6=kvbljiiils-kxbkrjbr.

Safer Foundation. http://www.saferfoundation.org/about/overview.

The Vice Lords Street Gang of Chicago. YouTube documentary 44:42. April 12, 2014. https://www.youtube.com/watch?v=UJkL-XuIg-U.